The Church
&The Parachurch

The Church & The Parachurch

An Uneasy Marriage

JERRY WHITE

MULTNOMAH PRESS
PORTLAND, OREGON 97266

Other books by Jerry White:

The Christian in Mid-Life, Jerry and Mary White
The Christian Student's How to Study Guide
Friends and Friendship: The Secrets of Drawing Closer,
Jerry and Mary White
Honesty, Morality and Conscience
Your Job: Survival or Satisfaction? Jerry and Mary White

Scripture quotations are from the Holy Bible: New International Version, © 1978 by the New York International Bible Society. Used by permission of Zondervan Bible Publishers.

Edited by Rod Morris
Cover design and illustration by Britt Taylor Collins

THE CHURCH & THE PARACHURCH
© 1983 by Multnomah Press
Portland, Oregon 97266

Printed in the United States of America

First Printing 1983

Library of Congress Cataloging in Publication Data

White, Jerry E., 1937-
    The church and the parachurch.

    Bibliography: p. 179
    Includes indexes.
    1. Religious and ecclesiastical institutions.   2. Church
I. Title.   II. Title: Parachurch.
BX2.W48   1983   261   83-12125
ISBN 0-88070-018-1

Contents

Appendixes

Preface

As I shared the topic of this book with pastors, parachurch staff, and lay people, their immediate responses ranged from a rolling of the eyes, to a sympathetic clucking of the tongue, to surprised looks of disbelief—or was it pity? I empathize with all of them.

The idea for this book came out of a lunch meeting with several Multnomah Press staff. They had asked me for book ideas, and I casually mentioned my thinking on the relationship of the church to the parachurch. Their response was immediate. They said the need was great and that it was urgent to address the issue—to get it out of the closet.

After prayer and reflection, I countered with the question, "Why produce a book that no one may like?" My fear was that it would not please *either* local church or parachurch proponents. But Critical Concern Books typically address the hard issues. Their purpose is to generate thinking and growth in the body of Christ.

Christianity is at a crossroads. The church in the second half of the twentieth century bears little resemblance to that of the first half. And one of the new dimensions is what I will term the "para-local church" movement. The proliferation of organizations outside the traditional boundaries of the local church is so great as to stagger the imagination. Its potential input can either divide or build the kingdom of God. We cannot turn back the calendar or re-write history. We must live where we are today. And the American church of today consists of multiple forms of church structure and non-local church organizations.

What qualifies me to tackle such a topic? I am a layman

turned vocational Christian worker, not a theologian. I serve in a para-local church organization, so would I not be biased? But then, would not a pastor also be biased?

I concluded that my background does lend to a fair treatment of the subject. I am a churchman, through and through. Since my high school days I have always been an active part of a local congregation, while at the same time I have been an active part of several other para-local church organizations—Youth for Christ, The Navigators, Officer's Christian Fellowship, Christian Service Brigade, and a Christian school board. I have struggled with the issues of the authority, legitimacy, and necessity of para-local church organizations.

In my adult years I have been an integral part of five local congregations and three military chapels. In the last two decades, I have served on two elder/deacon boards. I have never left a church for other than a geographical relocation, regardless of its growth pains and difficulties. Consequently, I speak from twenty-five years of personal experience as well as current extensive research and study.

In this book I represent my own views as applied to the broad spectrum of the para-local church societies, not the view of The Navigators as an organization.

As part of the research for this book, surveys were sent to one hundred pastors and twenty-five para-church organizations. Fifty-two pastors and twelve organizations responded. Their comments and views clarify many of the issues in a helpful way. Any material appearing in quotation marks is actual quotes altered only with grammatical clarification, since many comments in the surveys were incomplete sentences or abbreviated statements. These viewpoints will be presented in chapter 1 and appendix B.

I have avoided picking out specific local churches or para-local church organizations for analysis or evaluation. I have purposely restrained mentioning specific groups or churches unless they occurred in quotes from published works or an occasional personal illustration. My purpose is to deal with the issues, not personalities or organizations. Consequently, all unpublished quotes are anonymous whether they come from surveys or personal conversations.

My thanks and credit to Bernard Thompson (researcher, writer, editor) for his thorough literature search and extensive bibliography, as well as the compilation of the many surveys returned from pastors and organizational leaders (see appendix C for samples of those surveys). However, I assume full responsibility for all that is contained in this work.

It is with great desire, and some trepidation, that I present this study in the hope that it will prove to be a catalyst for understanding and mutual acceptance in the kingdom of God in our day.

An argument started among the disciples as to which of them would be the greatest. Jesus, knowing their thoughts, took a little child and had him stand beside him. Then he said to them, "Whoever welcomes this little child in my name welcomes me; and whoever welcomes me welcomes the one who sent me. For he who is least among you all—he is the greatest."

"Master," said John, "we saw a man driving out demons in your name and we tried to stop him, because he is not one of us."

"Do not stop him," Jesus said, "for whoever is not against you is for you."

Luke 9:46-50

Introduction

Who Is Doing the Work of the Kingdom?

The five men trooped through the hotel lobby at the end of the second day of the pastor's conference.

"Does anybody want a cup of hot chocolate or a banana split?"

"I need something," the oldest of the five said. "But I think it's a good night's sleep."

"Well, at least stop by my room for a ten minute rehash of the day."

The youngest of them gave a quick laugh. "If it's like last night's ten minute rehash, I'll get my pajamas on first."

All five filed into Paul and Tom's room and made themselves comfortable. After a few minutes of chit-chat, Charles, the gray-haired elder of the group, commented, "This is quite an ecumenical group. One Presbyterian, two Baptists, an independent, and a Free Church man. And we span quite a few years, too. Two of you just five years into your first pastorate. Two in midlife—and mid-career. And me—a couple of years beyond that. We ought to be able to cook up some wisdom if we put our minds to it."

"Well, I don't know about wisdom," said Paul. "But I do have a thought on this conference. I wish they'd have a workshop on how to contend with all these parachurch groups I run into. I'm just in the growing pains of my first church and that issue keeps coming up. I've got several key laymen involved in at least three different groups. How do you guys handle that?"

"I just ignore them and hope they'll go away," said Arnold. "But I don't think they will."

"Well," Marvin said with a broad smile, "you know the verse—'upon this rock I will build my parachurch.' " They all chuckled.

"Frankly," said Arnold with his jaw clenched, "I think they're leeches on the church in almost every way—financially, leadership, unity of the body—you name it! We have budget problems. If everyone in my church stopped giving to parachurch ministries and gave to the church, we'd be far over our budget. What's more, I have some excellent leaders who could carry a much bigger load, but they're too involved in other ministries. To top it off, the staff of these organizations have the nerve to come to our missions committee and ask for support!"

"Why don't you just turn down their request to come to the committee?" asked Marvin.

"I can't. There's too much pressure from some of my key people who've been helped by these groups in the past. So I just grin and bear it. I've tried to broach the subject with a few of them, but I can't really tell them how I feel."

"It's like that in my church too," Paul said. "What gets me is that there's such an insensitivity to the local church. Some of them almost bristle with pride at how much better they're doing things than the church. A friend of mine in our denomination feels they drain leadership from the local church. They become exclusive and display a superior attitude. Then they leave the hangers-on to the church. I know that may be a little strong, but I think he's right."

"Well," stated Arnold, "I really think they're unbiblical when they're not under the authority of the local church. They do the work the church should be doing—evangelism and discipleship. If they'd do it in the church it'd be biblical."

Charles raised one bushy eyebrow and said, "But Arnold, is the church doing what it should?"

"Probably not as well as we should. But we could do so much

better without the draining effect of these groups."

"My experience hasn't been too broad," said Paul, "but I do have a real question about the accountability of these parachurch groups. Who blows the whistle on them when they get out of bounds? Most of them have a very weak doctrinal position—watered down to try to please most churches."

"Most of them don't really help their people transfer to the church, so they flounder around inside the church expecting it to meet all the needs the parachurch group met." Marvin paused a moment and then continued, "In fact, many come into the church with a defensive, antichurch posture. I believe some of the parachurch staff really are antichurch, even though they're members of some local church. Do any of you have parachurch people in your churches?"

"Having had several churches," said Charles, "I guess I've seen both ends of the spectrum. Some parachurch staff made a superb contribution and served on our board. Others were a real pain in the neck. I used to get very tense about it, but over the years I've seen some fine people reached and brought into our church by these groups. The older groups seem to have learned their lessons and made some adjustments. But now the proliferation of organizations is so great that you can hardly make any generalizations."

Paul noticed that Tom had said very little. "Tom, you've been pretty quiet. Are you asleep?"

"No. I've been listening and thinking. It's a dilemma for me, too. But I have a special problem. I came to Christ through one of those groups, and I'm in the ministry today because of their part in my early Christian life. I get confused. I know I can't use my experience to justify their existence—but it does seem that God uses them. I find myself positive toward the one that helped me, and wary of the others. I do see the problem you men bring up."

"Maybe there'll get to be so many of them that they'll fight among themselves and. . . ."

"Point well made," said Marvin. "But something's got to give. We're sitting on a powder keg."

The discussion went on for another hour as the men dissected the role and doctrine of the church as it relates to the parachurch.

Finally, the discussion broke up with many opinions expressed, but with nothing changed.

At the same time these five pastors began their session, another one formed three floors below in the same hotel. This one was by appointment, not accident. Several parachurch staff were attending the conference and were meeting to discuss the church.

Ray was in his early forties and had been with one of the older parachurch organizations for fifteen years. Frank had recently joined a youth movement after serving in a small church as youth pastor. He was thirty-one. Alan was the only seminary graduate at the group and served with an independent mission agency. David was forty-five and had left a successful business career in his late thirties to work with a group that focused on reaching young, un-churched couples. Larry, at twenty-five, was the youngest and he worked with high school students.

"How are you enjoying the conference?" asked Ray.

"It's really great," said Frank. "And the fellowship is out-standing—until they find out I'm not working on a church staff. Then a polite frost sets in. If you'd told me when I was a youth pastor about that kind of reaction, I wouldn't have believed it."

"Join the crowd," cracked Alan. "Even my seminary training doesn't cut the ice with most pastors. They think I've wasted my education."

"That's why I thought it would be good to meet and talk," said Ray. "I wonder if there are some things we can do to change the atmosphere and attitude?"

"Nothing short of a miracle," said David. "Sometimes I think the church is more of a hindrance than a help. Most of the people I work with wouldn't darken the door of most churches. I tried for years to get them to come to my church. Finally I realized that I had to go to them. But I ran into real opposition with my pastor because my Bible studies were not in the church program and I used some parachurch materials."

"Maybe you were a little too aggressive or independent," commented Alan.

"Perhaps. But I saw a lot of people trust Christ for salvation. Some came to our church, and some went to other churches. But there was always a cloud of suspicion over what I did. When I wanted to go full-time, I tried to get our church to take me on. The pastor was polite, but buried the idea. So I finally went full-time with my current organization."

Larry tossed his shoes under the chair as if he were settling in for a long conversation. "I'm fed up with the whole thing. The pastor thinks he and his church are the only ones God is using. But it's almost pathetic to see the minor impact they're making on the unchurched or those in liberal churches. If it weren't for the fact that my leadership insists on our staff being in a church, I think I'd abandon it and start something that isn't crippled with traditional structures and an ingrown viewpoint of the kingdom of God."

"Larry, I think your youth and impatience are showing," commented Ray. "I know it can be frustrating when you don't quite fit into the church system, but it's important to keep trying and to keep the relationships. I suspect your perfect church would soon grow and get arthritis too."

"You're probably right, Ray. But their viewpoint is so narrow. There's so much more to do than to hassle about who's doing the work of God and who gets the credit."

"There's some truth to what Larry is saying," David observed. "I've been deep in both structures. I know I used to feel a keen sense of competition from parachurch groups when I was on the elder board. I wish now I'd known how to work with them and include them more."

Frank shifted in his chair as he began to speak. "I guess I'm really the fortunate one here. I have a tremendous relationship with my church. But it wasn't always like that. Until we hired our current pastor, my whole ministry was under suspicion. But this new man really considers me a part of the outreach of the church, even though they don't expect operational authority over me. I look to them for personal accountability. They support me financially, and encourage me and my family with prayer. We're really part of their missionary family."

"You're one of the few," Alan observed. "You must have a very secure pastor. Many pastors aren't broad enough in their thinking to include people like you."

"Well, I think it's time for a little testimony," Ray said as he got up from his chair and sat on the edge of the desk. "A number of years ago I was really upset with the church. I had some bad experiences—and I'm sure I was impetuous and didn't earn my right to be heard. But I was fast becoming antichurch in my attitude. Then my kids became teenagers. It was the church that ministered to them, not my organization. Ann became ill, and the church rallied around us. I suddenly saw where I really needed them. I've changed my attitude a lot. I still get frustrated at some narrow thinking, but I tolerate it better."

"I can see your point," agreed David, "but do they support you in your work any more than they did before?"

"Well, some do. I think much of the support is because we're really a part of the church. I don't think their thinking has changed conceptually. In fact, I suspect that if we moved to another community they wouldn't continue our financial support. In principle, they support only missionaries from their own denominational mission agencies."

"I know staff of other organizations who've simply given up on most local churches," Larry said. "They're meeting in small fellowships that they feel meet the real needs of most of the people they work with."

"In many ways, they're right," observed David. "When we reach people who have no church background, bringing them to our standard evangelical church is a real stumbling block to their growth. They puzzle over the language and terminology. They don't know the hymns. Much of what goes on is over their heads or irrelevant to their needs. They have no idea how to break into the system. It takes almost six months for them to begin to feel comfortable—and most bail out before that. I know the local church doesn't intend that to happen, but it does."

Alan nodded agreement. "When I was on church staff, that was a constant frustration. But did you ever try to change the format of service, structure, or meetings in a church? It's almost as hard as changing the United States Constitution. There are so many areas where the church simply doesn't have the resources to specialize and reach out. Parachurch groups can focus their entire attention on certain specific areas."

"From my experience with many parachurch staff, and many churches and pastors," Ray said, "one of the key issues is money. There's never enough to go around. The church needs more. The parachurch needs more. The church suspects that the parachurch doesn't use the funds well. And parachurch groups feel that the church pours too much money into its buildings rather than missions and people. The church believes all monies should go through the local church, and the parachurch knows they could never exist if that were the case. That problem will not be solved easily, but I think it underlies much of the conflict. It's more volatile than a simple theological argument on the legitimacy of the existence of the parachurch."

"But what's the answer?" asked David. "Live and let live?"

"I wish I knew," mused Ray. "The status quo is not feasible. I believe a crisis will come soon that will either unify or produce a greater rift between local churches and parachurch groups. The world's view of Christianity is already shaky enough without more conflict—especially in evangelical circles."

In the back rooms and board rooms, criticism, competition, and complaining run rampant.

Is this simply the logical extension of the historic tension between church denominations? Or is it something new?

No one ever genuinely welcomes competition. The neighborhood grocer seldom puts up posters welcoming the new supermarket opening down the street. Nor do churches welcome a new parachurch organization or even a new church into their area.

The vying for people and money, though not the sole cry of battle, is certainly a key part of the conflict. Theology? Yes, it is there, too, but not as clearly as we might think. After all, theology brought that new church into the area—or was it really theology? Perhaps it was the family that didn't like the youth program or had a conflict with the pastor in their previous church.

What causes a new ministry which does the same thing as our church, to spring up? Some theological differences, some methodology differences, some goal differences (at least in theory)—but mostly just differences between people. Why don't we get together? We both want to reach the lost, or the neighborhood, or the college. The answer is often crystal clear to a few of the people directly involved, and a great mystery to most others.

Twenty years ago, many pastors viewed the parachurch as a temporary phenomenon or a small irritant needed to spur the church to renewal. Today the exploding number and power of parachurch groups appear to be a permanent and growing fixture in the evangelical community as it approaches the twenty-first century. The parachurch cannot be ignored. Nor can the parachurch ignore the local church.

What can be done? Neither local churches nor parachurch societies speak with one voice. We must approach the issues with wisdom, understanding, and a deep desire to see God's kingdom advanced. It is unlikely that any corporate expression or resolution can have a significant effect. The basic solution lies with individual staff in the church and the parachurch.

Many issues are raised by the pastors and parachurch staff in the dialogue at the beginning of this introduction. Those issues, along with many others, will be highlighted in the next chapter. Stephen Board stresses their importance: "As these organizations have grown, the clergy and church leaders have wondered if the tail has begun wagging the dog. In influence and money—that is, in power—the parachurch agencies are running away with the ballgame."[1]

Although we could debate the accuracy of this assertion, it nevertheless emphasizes the growing perception the evangelical community has of the emergence and prominence of the parachurch. Silence, quiet concern, or private critique are no longer adequate. We must address the issues and propose realistic solutions.

Who is really doing the work of the kingdom? The church? The parachurch? Both?

DEFINITION

To this point in the book, I have simply assumed that the term parachurch communicated adequately. In fact, there is not universal agreement or understanding. We need a definition for use in this study.

The prefix "para" means "along side of, by, near." Thus, the term parachurch means "along side of the church." But what is the church? Is it the local congregation, a denomination, or the body of Christ made up of all believers (the universal church)?

To avoid this confusion as well as to clarify the issues, we will use the term "para-local church."[2] This designation is less ambiguous and, as will be shown in chapter 3, more accurately describes the relationship and function of organizations whose primary ministry is outside the direct authority of local congregations. Whenever the term "church" or "local church" is used, it means a local congregation. Universal church or body of Christ will be used to designate the fellowship of all believers. So our working definition will be:

> *Para-local church:* Any spiritual ministry whose organization is not under the control or authority of a local congregation.

This definition and a breakdown of types of para-local church structures will be developed in chapter 3.

Introduction, Notes

1. Stephen Board, "The Great Evangelical Power Shift," *Eternity*, June 1979, p. 17.

2. I first heard the term "para-local church" used by Lorne Sanny, president of The Navigators.

PART
1

GAINING PERSPECTIVE ON
THE PROBLEMS AND ISSUES

*"The first to present his case
seems right, till another comes forward
and questions him."*
Proverbs 18:17

Chapter 1

Personal Perspectives

Viewpoints differ radically according to one's circumstances, training, and experience. A farmer and an industrial worker view legislation differently. An employee and an employer view wages differently. Students and teachers view education differently. We all tend to look at events and circumstances through the peephole in the wall of our own position and involvement.

Because of this, we would expect pastors and church laymen to view the growing para-local church movement through different eyes than para-local church staff and their constituents. The results of the research conducted for this book confirm these expectations.

THE PERSPECTIVE OF THE LOCAL CHURCH

We encounter a wide variation of viewpoints among pastors toward para-local church groups. (See appendix B, for example, for suggested reasons by pastors for the proliferation of such groups.) Some pastors are very tolerant and make efforts to encourage para-local church staff and organizations. Others are strongly opposed even to those organizations' existence. Obviously, local churches do not speak with one voice. The variation results from experience, theology, and a number of pragmatic considerations such as money and people.

Many pastors believe para-local church organizations usurp what the local church should do. They believe para-local church groups are "taking responsibilities that belong to the churches."

Some pastors feel that para-local church groups fail "to realize that the local church is the primary channel God uses to evangelize the world." Or, as another forcefully pointed out, "Where parachurch organizations are not tied in with the local church, they are *unbiblical.*"

In a similar vein was the criticism that para-local church groups "promote themselves above local church ministry, bypassing the authority of the local church and its leaders in counseling young Christians, and make token efforts at attendance . . . A.M. services but not P.M. or midweek prayer." Another felt that para-local church groups "take the focus off the local body which is God's vessel for this age. The spiritual gifts were for the local church and to be used in that context."

These expressions are representative of a segment of pastors who place primary emphasis on the local congregation, questioning both the existence and certainly the effectiveness of any group outside the auspices of the local church. Even where there is tolerance of para-local church ministries, these same feelings stir beneath the surface.

Many pastors spoke of the quality, style, and effectiveness of the ministry of para-local church groups. One commented that a para-local church group "develops such a strong small-group relatedness, unduplicatable in many churches, that church seems too tame or irrelevant. The result is that many members of the parachurch groups are constantly, sometimes unconsciously, seeking for the same thing, and so unable or unwilling to develop such relationships in the communion in which the Lord has placed them." This fact, along with many other distinctive characteristics of para-local church organizations, puts pressure on the local congregation to become like them or at least to provide similar programs and experiences. Yet most churches cannot do this and still minister to the broad mix of people in their congregations.

This specialized, focused nature of para-local church groups confines their effectiveness to a small segment of the body of Christ. The local church views the para-local church as unable to meet the broad spiritual, social, and personal needs of most of the people in their congregations.

Some pastors believe para-local church organizations do not have an appreciation for the whole body. "They minister to a select group rather than a broad spectrum. This can be their strength if they don't try to be a substitute for the church." Another commented that para-local church groups "give a narrow scope of God's work—only the committed—and may not have a concern for the bulk of Christians who need encouragement to get to a committed level." The problem is not that the para-local church specializes, but that they do not recognize the broader scope of needs in the church.

Some, in fact, believe that para-local church groups tend to remove the very people who could help meet many of these broader needs. They sense that the para-local church has the "potential to drain leadership from local churches, to become exclusive and manifest a superior attitude, and to cream the crop, leaving hangers-on to the church."

Some accuse the specialized para-local church staff of having "tunnel vision." "When they come into the local church setting, their blinders keep them from seeing the larger scope of the ministry church staff are attempting to accomplish and then misunderstandings occur."

These are strong feelings and highlight the tension between the specialist nature of para-local church organizations and the generalist nature of the local church.

Some pastors stress the need for accountability of para-local church staff and organizations to the local church. They see "many individuals wanting to do their own thing without any accountability." They also see "young, though enthusiastic, leadership without adequate grounding or accountability." Some pastors believe that any authority structure beyond or outside the local church level is illegitimate.

No critique or summary of criticism would be complete without mentioning finances. Especially during times of economic trials, money stirs emotions. Many pastors feel that para-local church groups drain the church of finances that should go to the local church. One pastor complained, "They seem to take the local church for granted. For example, they will recruit a person from a campus and often when that person is ready to leave for his service, they will ask the church for support. At times we wonder if organizations want anything besides our money." Another pastor expressed that para-local church staff were "using the church" only to gain financial support.

Next to finances, the biggest point of contention is people. People run the church and the para-local church. One pastor stated that the "local church ministry is gravely weakened" because the para-local church "diverts resources and personnel." Others sensed a "dilution of church leadership and of member loyalty." Not everyone possesses the capacity to do many things well, so choices must be made. For some, these choices leave the local church low on the list of priorities. When that occurs, conflicts arise or bad feelings develop.

Some pastors believe para-local church groups are weak in their doctrinal position and in their presentation of salvation. Since para-local church groups must relate to a wide range of evangelical churches, they are less precise and outspoken about their doctrinal stand. This gives some the impression that they "weaken their doctrinal position to attract a wider constituency."

Many pastors (even those who point out problems) are very positive toward the continuation of para-local church groups. One wrote, "Who are we seeking to reach with the gospel? The parachurch group generally has a closer relationship with non-Christians outside the church—and the problem is the slow and long trek back to the church—the parachurch workers need to see this as part of their task, and the church needs to welcome their help." Another said, "Our church has benefited greatly by the ministries and gifts of many committed parachurch people. Many have made a significant contribution to the body here. I have seen a shift in the last ten years in some organizations toward cooperation with the local church."

Pastors and church staff generally regard the para-local

church movement as a mixed blessing. The movement spurs the church to re-examine its effectiveness in many areas. Yet it creates a measure of conflict and competition not unlike that of the historical conflict between churches of various denominations within a given city. In some cases para-local church staff are welcomed for their participation and contribution in a local congregation, and in other cases they are simply tolerated or given a cold shoulder. The tendency among pastors is to evaluate para-local church groups on the basis of their contribution to *their* local church. Contribution to other local churches was seldom mentioned. There was little thought of other local churches as a part of their church's mission or concern.

THE PERSPECTIVE OF THE PARA-LOCAL CHURCH

An interesting phenomenon arose in surveying para-local church leaders. Almost no one made any derogatory or critical comments about the local church. While individual pastors were unusually outspoken, para-local church leaders were uniformly positive in their comments. Yet, in many cases, real undercurrents of dissatisfaction formed the foundational impetus in starting a para-local church organization. Para-local church leaders obviously think their organizations are needed to accomplish something the church cannot or will not do. What then is behind this lack of public criticism?

Several issues can be identified. Para-local church groups cannot afford (or at least will not risk) the public relations problems arising from criticism of the local church. It would be akin to criticizing "motherhood and apple pie" in the United States. Para-local church groups need and want the support of the local church.

Another factor is that most of the surveys were sent to *leaders* who spoke for their organizations rather than for themselves. Had I surveyed individual staff members, as I surveyed individual pastors, some strong viewpoints probably would have surfaced. Also, most leaders seriously believe they are part of the local church and want to build up the local congregations.

Because para-local church leaders are hesitant to publicly

criticize the local church, I will supply (without benefit of direct quotes) some of the key problems I have heard mentioned or that I know are felt by some para-local church staff.

Many para-local church staff believe that large segments of the U.S. population are virtually untouched, and even untouchable, by local evangelical congregations and denominations. A generation ago, many people had some acquaintance with the Bible and church, but that has changed. The continuing secularization of our society effectively places large numbers of people outside the influence of the local church. They reject the idea of church and have no biblical background to draw on even to understand a brief presentation of the gospel. People in nonevangelical churches are even more isolated from a local evangelical congregation and other evangelical influences.

Who reaches out to students, business people, secularized young people, blue-collar workers, ethnic groups, and others who will not respond easily to organized religion? Many para-local church groups believe they target such segments with much greater effectiveness than any one local church can. A church that fosters study groups and witnessing efforts *unrelated* to and *uncontrolled* by the church can have an input. But most churches want their label attached to these efforts, and the evangelistic increase added to their congregation.

Worldwide, the situation is even more dramatic. Much of the great missionary movement of the last one hundred years was fostered by nondenominational groups. In the areas of social relief, evangelism, and church planting, para-local church organizations have taken the lead and initiative.

Many para-local church staff believe that the local church functions as a generalized ministry while neglecting or being unable to meet many specialized needs of Christians. Most para-local church groups specialize their efforts in some way by concentrating on evangelism, discipleship, counseling, translation, or publishing, or by working with ethnic groups, children, military personnel, students, or hidden people. And this list is by no means exhaustive. Only the largest of churches can afford to promote and staff such specialized ministries. Therefore, many of these needs would go largely unmet without the para-local church.

A criticism often heard is that the church is too program- and building-oriented. Anything that does not fit the program of the local congregation simply receives no support—even for the layman who wants to have a specialized ministry. The internal machinery of approval for new efforts becomes so laborious that tradition and programing rule the day. The church largely takes on the function of an educational institution rather than an organized body of believers. Except in a few rare churches, "we've never done that before" stifles most innovation.

Many para-local church people find that the church is too parochial and narrow in viewpoint and concern. The emphasis too often is on the work of one church, its building and programs, rather than on the kingdom of God. Separatism and denominationalism have left their divisive mark on the church.

The multiplicity of many Baptist groups, many Presbyterian groups, many independent churches, and more, confuses even most Christians. Churches split over doctrinal issues and contend over almost any controversial issue. Such narrowness mitigates against a strong outreach to the world, especially when specialized efforts beyond the capacity of most local congregations are needed. Church strategy is usually predicated not on whether a congregation exists in a given neighborhood, but whether one of "our brand" exists there.

Significant numbers of para-local church staff are lay people without formal theological training. They observe that the church is unable to adequately train and mobilize lay people in significant numbers to accomplish meaningful tasks. So much effort is expended on "manning the machinery" of the church organization that other needs are rarely addressed. Lay people are admonished to witness, but not taught how. They hear personal growth stressed, but do not know where to begin. When laymen want to minister, they go outside the local church to express their gifts—especially when they attempt to reach specialized segments of society or do specialized ministries. The attractiveness to laymen has been a significant factor in the growth of para-local church groups.

Some para-local church staff observe that many churches do

not give training and development to lay leaders. Rather they "use" capable people to fill the churches' needs for Sunday school teachers, ushers, committee members, and other positions. Para-local church members believe that most churches' idea of training is to "put them to work."

In general, para-local church staff believe they are making a significant contribution to the kingdom of God, and that their existence is completely legitimate. They would deny the theological argument put forward in some church circles that all ministry must be under the direct authority of the church. They are concerned at the lack of acceptance of their ministry even when, in many cases, that ministry would not—even could not—be done by the local church. Again, the specter of narrowness and self-centeredness surfaces. Such feelings actually drive para-local church people away from the church instead of drawing them and their fruit into the church.

On the positive side, para-local church leaders expressed a deep commitment to the local church. They desire the fruit of their ministries to be in the church, and their staff are encouraged to be an active part of a local congregation. Many have found great acceptance and a significant ministry in their churches as well as in their organizations. They recognize the need for the church to minister generally to the total body rather than to a specialized part. In fact, para-local church staff often develop new appreciation for the ministry of the church to their families when their children reach their teens.

THE ISSUES

You undoubtedly have felt some emotional reactions—both positive and negative—to many of the statements in this chapter. Each statement could be challenged and countered. Yet they represent real feelings on both sides of the issue. We need to accept them at their face value as expressions of concern and opinion, not as documented, defensible statements of fact. Most controversies are formed more on feeling than on fact—in churches, between churches, and certainly between the local church and the para-local church.

Four critical issues emerge from this study of local church and para-local church perspectives. They are leadership, legitimacy, money (loot, to alliterate!), and loyalties. Although these will be developed further in later chapters, a brief summary here will help focus our thinking on the subject.

PEOPLE (LEADERSHIP)

Every ministry has its major commodity—people. And of these people, leaders are always at a premium. Both the local church and para-local church groups need them. Usually one person cannot handle a deep involvement in both structures. Choices must be made—choices that often cause hard feelings and create conflict.

THEOLOGY (LEGITIMACY)

The theological questions of the legitimacy of para-local church organizations persist with some pastors and theologians. The basic argument against the existence of para-local church groups is that all legitimate functions must be under the authority or control of the church (either local or denominational, depending on one's ecclesiology). Few, if any, para-local church societies meet this requirement. The alternate view contends that we are all members of the body of Christ. Therefore para-local church members should be individually part of a local congregation, but their ministry does not need to be under its control to be legitimate.

FINANCES (MONEY)

No issue is quite so volatile as money. It divides friends and churches. But no organization (local church or para-local church) can function without it. Churches often feel that para-local church groups siphon off contributions that are rightfully theirs. Many subscribe to "storehouse tithing"—the idea that one's tithe must be brought to the storehouse (the church). Para-local church groups agree that all should give to the local church, but not to it exclusively. Because storehouse tithing is an Old Testament concept, they deny its direct application today and emphasize the need to support the broader ministry of the body of Christ. The bare fact remains that if para-local church groups were dependent on churches for their total support, there would be no para-local church groups! The majority of para-local church support comes from individuals, not churches. So competition for money becomes intense, especially in severe economic times.

AUTHORITY (LOYALTIES)

As people make choices about their spiritual involvements, they also encounter conflicts in spiritual authority. This issue is related to the theological question of legitimacy, but addresses a more specific aspect. Under whose authority does a Christian function in the exercise of his spiritual ministry? The local church? The para-local church group? Both?

Other issues that could be mentioned are exercise of gifts, duplication of ministries, doctrinal differences, and effectiveness. However, these lack the significance of the four discussed above.

*"Be careful that you do not forget
the LORD, who brought you out of Egypt,
out of the land of slavery."*
Deuteronomy 6:12

*"Remember the days of old;
consider the generations long past.
Ask your father and he will tell you,
your elders, and they will explain to you."*
Deuteronomy 32:7

Chapter 2

A Historical Perspective

*T*he proliferation of para-local church movements and organizations will be one of the distinguishing hallmarks of the last half of the twentieth century. Para-local church groups now number between five thousand and ten thousand, and that number is increasing daily. Some estimates run as high as twenty thousand. An accurate account defies research as many para-local church societies are virtually unknown, one or two person nonprofit agencies. Larger para-local church organizations number less than one thousand and generally are open to public scrutiny. Stephen Board reports some sixty-five hundred groups counting both Protestant and Catholic.[1] In perspective, this compares to 20,800 denominations (not local churches) in the world.[2]

Some view this proliferation with alarm, others with guarded delight. Some panic as they view the dwindling influence of the church in our society in favor of some growing nonchurch influences. Others simply see para-local church influence as a passing fad that will fade with time. But no one can ignore the trend.

"As these organizations have grown, the clergy and church leaders have wondered if the tail has begun wagging the dog. In influence and money—that is, in *power*—the parachurch agencies are running away with the ballgame. Their critics, usually pastors, charge them with imbalance, doctrinal indifference, and exploitations of congregations for money and people. The major criticism, and one that is easiest to make stick, is that they lack accountability to anyone but themselves. Parachurch groups are religion gone free enterprise."[3]

In light of such views, we cannot bury our heads and wish the conflict would go away. Perhaps if we trace some of the history of the para-local church and identify some of the reasons for its growth, we can better understand where it fits today.

In the following historical summary I will show the infant beginnings of the para-local church movement from the Pietists in 1669. Before this time there is no clear thread of such movements. However, the causes for the rise of such movements were evident much earlier. The history prior to 1600 primarily demonstrates the growing hierarchical structure, the resistance to change, and the increasing separation of clergy and laity. These issues, along with political and social corruption in the Roman Catholic Church of that time, contributed significantly to the beginnings of the Reformation. Thus the pre-Reformation history focuses on these themes.

PRIOR TO A.D. 250

In the first century, we see the fledgling body of Christ struggling to organize itself in the midst of opposition and oppression. Local congregations in various forms, sizes, and structures began to form. At the same time, mobile teams of missionaries spread outward with the dispersion, evangelizing both Jews and Gentiles. Local congregations began to form in Gentile cities. Their form and structure varied somewhat from culture to culture, and began to crystallize as Christianity became acceptable in a given city. Their form was significantly influenced by the Jewish synagogue structure and the order of the Graeco-Roman world.[4]

From the beginning, conflict erupted and began to divide the infant church between Jews and Gentiles, between conflicting doctrines of law and grace, and between the authority structures in Jerusalem and local cities. We see many expressions of the body of

Christ developing, meeting varying and specific needs in many geographical areas.

Ralph Winter claims that the earliest functioning missionary expressions were mobile functions and specialists similar to some para-local church groups today. They were related to, but not exclusively controlled by, the local congregations.

Paul founded several local congregations, but the Scriptures do not indicate that he was under the authority of any. Paul and Barnabas were certainly sent from the church at Antioch (Acts 13:1-3) as well as "by the Holy Spirit" (Acts 13:4). Yet in later years he does not seem to remain under their authority. His Jerusalem visit was more defensive than directive (Acts 15:1-29). Though the letter from the Jerusalem church (vv. 23-29) may seem directive, it really was permissive—and still infused with legalism. Paul's view of the visit was not particularly high (Galatians 2:1-10). "As for those who seemed to be important—whatever they were makes no difference to me; God does not judge by external appearance—those men added nothing to my message" (Galatians 2:6). Later he confronted Peter (reputed to be a pillar of the Jerusalem church, v. 9) for his personal hypocrisy (Galatians 2:11-14). Paul followed a rather indistinct line of authority. Or was he his own authority, responsible to the Holy Spirit?

Paul was an apostle with definite apostolic authority. Some claim that we cannot use him as a pattern. Others use him as a primary pattern in many areas of missionary endeavor and church structure. Here I simply note that Paul, as well as Barnabas and other New Testament missionaries, was not solely under the authority of a specified local church.[5]

In the generations immediately following the apostles, churches began to create structure to communicate with other churches on matters of discipline and doctrine. Men like Clement (an elder in Rome) and Ignatius of Antioch were among several whose writings about the early church have survived. Ignatius first taught the submission of leaders in local congregations to a ruling bishop.[6] Other writers, reflecting the trend, were Polycarp, Papias, Irenaeus, and Cyprian.

These writings reflect the early struggle to agree on doctrine and structure. Many of the ideas would seem heretical to us. Early heresies and subsequent conflict centered around the deity of Christ, infusion of pagan practices into Christian worship, the trinity, law versus grace, the doctrine of salvation (including priestly mediation and sacraments), and church authority and structure. The earliest of these heresies was gnosticism which, among other things, undermined the true deity and humanity of Christ.

Thus, for our purposes, we see the beginnings of local church definition and great variety in its expression during this early period. It was characterized by doctrinal and structural conflict that forced or precipitated significant unification and authoritative structure.

But in such unification and structure we see problems developing for the future. Restrictiveness and internal controversy caused a decreased effectiveness, but also forced a purifying of doctrine and orthodoxy.

A.D. 250 TO 590

In these three centuries, Christianity made both great strides forward and great mistakes. The most significant positive event was the development of the canon of the New Testament, which was finalized by the Council of Carthage in A.D. 397. The most significant detriment was the structural rigidity setting in through the establishment of a final human authority in the church, and the consequent deviation in the doctrine of salvation as taught by the infant Roman Catholic church.

From A.D. 260 to 303, persecution almost disappeared. Then came ten years of unprecedented and unparalleled persecution. Martyrdom was the norm. But Christianity had arrived to stay. People died violent deaths and many lived under intense persecution. Finally, out of this tribulation, Constantine made Christianity a legal religion in A.D. 313.

During these centuries, heretical sects sprang up one after another, causing much inner turmoil in the church. But these groups forced the fledgling church to focus back on the apostolic writings which later were to form the New Testament. Now authority rested in these Scriptures.

In the early years, the conflicts were either about doctrine or practice. Doctrine reflected what was believed in the church. Practice reflected how people structured and performed the work of the church.

Early in its history, the church began to divide into groups similar to denominations. One of these was the Novatian Schism in A.D. 251. The issue was the forgiveness of those who had succumbed under the recent Decian persecution. The schismatic group called themselves *Katharoi* or Puritans. They chose Novatian as their bishop. He "argued that the church had no power to grant forgiveness to those guilty of murder, adultery or apostacy. It could only intercede for God's mercy at the last Judgment." They formed a "network of small congregations and considered the Catholic churches polluted. . . ."[7] The main stream of Catholicism initiated a sacrament of penance and the church administered forgiveness.

Another early division bore some similarity to Luther's and other later Reformer's protests against an immoral clergy. They were called Donatists, after an early bishop of Carthage (Donatus [313-355]). "The movement stood for a holy church, for church discipline, and for the unflinching resistance of unworthy bishops. The Donatists said the Catholics had surrendered all of these by ordaining immoral priests and bishops."[8] Thus in North Africa, about fifty years after the Novatian Schism, a new division split from the Catholic Church.

These are examples of the seemingly continuous conflicts and divisions in the church.

It is in this period also that we see the view of church and papal authority developing. One of the earliest statements came from Cyprian, another bishop of Carthage and an opponent of the Novatians. He declared, "The invariable source of heresies and schisms is in refusal to obey the priest of God [the bishop], the failure to have one in the church who is looked upon as the temporal representative of Christ as priest and judge."[9] A tighter concept of authority then continues to develop in the church from this point till the Reformation.

A.D. 590 TO 1305

This period of church history begins with Gregory the Great (540-604), a former mayor of Rome who was never comfortable with secular power, but preferred the meager life of a monk. His writings and decisions set the course of the Roman Catholic church for this entire period. He sent forty monks to England in 597 in a missionary endeavor. He was acclaimed a "universal pope." He taught the intercession of saints for the people, the veneration of holy relics (the remains of martyrs and saints), and the concept of purgatory. He also became a powerful political leader. "After Gregory, the pope was no longer only a Christian leader; he was also an important political figure in European politics—God's consul."[10]

The period ended in 1305 with the appointment of Pope Clement V who ruled from Avignon, France, rather than Rome. The period also culminated with that dark blot on Christian history, the medieval Crusades.

The history of the Christian church marches through these years with growing consolidation of earthly papal power, personified in Innocent III. With it we see the ignominious rise of political intrigue and involvement on the part of clergy. Divisive forces continued to break out from within and unrelenting attacks came from without. Yet in the midst of turmoil there were undoubtedly faithful people who quietly practiced true Christianity while the majority were "Christianized" in a legalistic and politically motivated sense.

Many major events scarred this period. In the 600s, Islam developed and began to ravage the Middle East, North Africa, and Southern Europe. In 800, the Holy Roman Empire was born and remained a political power with a Christian facade until Napoleon abolished it in 1806.

The papacy and the organization of the Roman Catholic church developed to a focused and effective hierarchy and authority. Their power was shown at its zenith in the infamous Crusades (1095-1291). Sparked by the Turkish conquest of Palestine, four major Crusades mercilessly spilled blood in the name of Christianity. Much of the motivation was political as well as religious. Power and authority over the people motivated the medieval papacy. In 1215 (the Fourth Lateran Council), annual confession to a priest was made mandatory for all laymen. The Council also affirmed the dogma of transubstantiation which asserts that the priest performs an actual sacrifice of Christ every time the mass is said.

In this period of medieval decline, deviation from prescribed views was squelched with fear and violence. As many attempted to reform the practices of the church, they were opposed on every front by the organized church. The early Inquisition of 1000-1300 attempted to crush dissidents by political authority, accompanied by claims of innocence on the part of the church. An early target of the Inquisition is reported by Durant. "About the year 1000 a sect appeared in Toulouse and Orleans which denied the reality of miracles, the regenerative virtue of baptism, the presence of Christ in the Eucharist and the efficacy of prayers to the saints. They were ignored for a time, then condemned; and thirteen of their number were burned at the stake in 1023."[11] These issues were early preludes to the Reformation.

Durant reports that many of these people were anticlerical. "Some were harmless groups who gathered to read the Bible to one another in the vernacular without a priest, and to put their own 'interpretation' upon its disputed passages. . . . The Franciscan movement arose as such a sect, and narrowly escaped being classed as heretical."[12]

A key anticleric and prereformer, Peter Waldo (1140-1218), was finally excommunicated and many of his followers were martyred. Waldo had portions of the Bible translated into the vernacular French, and he taught a life of poverty and a pooling of resources for subsistance. "Peter went to Rome (1179) and asked Alexander III for a preaching license. It was granted, on condition of consent and supervision of local clergy. Peter resumed his preaching, apparently without such local consent. His followers became devotees of the Bible, and learned large sections of it by heart. Gradually the movement took on an antisacerdotal tinge, rejected all priesthood, denied the validity of sacraments administered by a sinful priest, and attributed to every believer in a state of sanctity the power to forgive sins."[13]

Pope Alexander III did not pronounce the Waldenses heretical; "they were mere laymen, however, so he ruled that they could preach only by the invitation of bishops, a very unlikely prospect."[14] We note here the beginnings of not just a reformation, but of a *movement of laymen carrying on a personal ministry outside the direct authority and control of the church.* This is similar to a major emphasis of today's para-local church groups—the involvement of the laity.

Not long after Waldo, St. Francis of Assisi, another layman, led a new movement. Innocent III in 1209, unlike the treatment of Waldo, approved Francis and his band of Friars Minor, known to us today as Franciscans. Waldo and Francis illustrate the two options for reform or lay movements. The former was forced out to form another organization; the latter was included and approved as an "order."

The decline of true Christianity in the Roman Catholic church in both clergy and laity is understood better after considering the comments of the noted church historian, Kenneth Scott Latourette.

> Not infrequently mass conversion was hastened by the use of force. For instance, more than one Scandinavian king resorted to arms to defend himself against the pagan opposition or to overwhelm the recalcitrants. Often baptism was imposed as a sign of submission to a foreign conqueror. A Christian monarch in seeking to extend his domains sought to assimilate his new subjects to his religion and required baptism and, perhaps, the support of Christian clergy. . . .
>
> The fact that conversions were so largely the result of group action under the direction of civil authorities made for a very superficial and formal Christianity. At the outset few had even an inkling of the original nature of that which they were accepting. When they learned more about it, it was chiefly from monks. The current Christianity, therefore, strongly smacked of monastic

ideals. The perfect Christian, thus the belief ran, was the ideal monk. Not for centuries, and then not everywhere, did a lay Christianity develop which held to another view of faith. Slowly the masses acquired more knowledge of the faith. Increasingly in Europe Christianity was woven into the fabric of life and culture. Yet never did it entirely escape from the consequences of the method of its introduction. Only the minorities, whether of lay folk, or of monks, or of clergy, entered whole-heartedly into the inward spirit of Christianity as it was preached and lived in the ancient world by the greatest of the early disciples.[15]

Consequently excesses, heresies, rebellion, and attempted reform should be of little surprise against this backdrop of history. The stage is now set for both the Reformation and the insurgence of laymen into the ministry of the church.

A.D. 1305 TO 1648

This period of history is characterized by two major events—Renaissance and Reformation. Volumes have been written on these eras. But we must confine ourselves to the ideas that most pertain to the topic at hand—the formation and concept of the local church as we see it today, and the involvement of people and movements outside or alongside the local church.

John Wycliffe (1310-1384) led a succession of reformers culminating in Luther's symbolic act of defiance at Wittenberg in 1517. Wycliffe was an Oxford-educated priest. He led in the translation of the first English version of the Bible. He instructed and sent out lay evangelists. He was part of an anticlerical movement that resisted both the growing wealth of the church and its declining morals. Wycliffe's theology, though long preceding Calvin's, was ultra-Calvinistic in its view of predestination. He opposed the infallibility of the pope, and stressed the Bible as the sole unerring guide to true religion. His followers, known as Lollards, spread widely in Britain and then Europe. Wycliffe was ultimately censored and condemned for his opposition to the Roman Catholic church.

John Hus (1369-1415) of Bohemia fought against indulgences (payment for services or privileges) to the pope, as well as subscribing to much of Wycliffe's teaching. He was popular, leading a significant reform movement. He declared that the church was all the saved, clergy and laity. In 1415, he was imprisoned by Pope John XXIII (antipope), and then burned at the stake as he chanted hymns. A Bohemian revolution ensued, led by the "Husites." Other Protestant-like sects came out of the Husite groups.

During this age of Renaissance, knowledge grew rapidly and explorers like Columbus searched the seas. It was also a time of political, social, and economic unrest. Humanism and an academic emphasis began to captivate the minds of learned men. The Roman Catholic church was plagued by simony, immorality, and the purchase of salvation.

Upon this scene came Martin Luther following the path of Wycliffe and Hus. He sought for change in the church, not separation. His goal was not to start a new movement. But like a match near dry tinder, the fire of Reformation caught on quickly and far exceeded anything he had expected. The act of nailing his ninety-five theses to the door of the Wittenberg church was simply a protest against the sale of indulgences. It became the first of a series of events which culminated with his appearance before the Diet of Worms in 1521, where he said, "I cannot and will not recant anything, since it is neither safe nor honest to act against one's conscience. God help me. Amen."

Sometime in 1508 or 1509, as a pious and legalistic monk, he encountered Romans 1:17 and the phrase, "The just shall live by faith." His terror of judgment was relieved in the dual concept of faith and predestination. Some believe this was his time of salvation. During the period from 1512-17, he began to leave the official doctrine of the church as he began to teach the Bible. The accusations against him at the Diet of Worms were harsh: "This devil in the habit of a monk has brought together ancient errors into one stinking puddle, and has invented new ones."[16] But the Reformation had begun. Nine years after Luther died, following a Protestant-Catholic war, the Diet of Augsburg (1555) recognized both Catholicism and Lutheranism as legal religions in Europe.

Other movements were developing as well. Ulrich Zwingli (1484-1531) in German speaking Switzerland; John Calvin (1509-1564) in France, Germany, and Switzerland; the Huguenots in France (spilling into England, Holland, and Prussia); the secession of the English church under Henry VIII; the Puritans in England; George Wishart and John Knox in Scotland; William of Orange in Holland; and many free church movements, with the Anabaptists as forerunners.

Latourette records that the Anabaptists (Again-baptizers or Re-baptizers) had no single spokesman. "[The movement] traced its spiritual descent from some of the groups, usually of humble folk, of the Middle Ages, who, touched by the New Testament, attempted to reproduce what they believed to be the simplicity and the thoroughgoing commitment of life to the Christian ideal characteristic of Christians of Apostolic times."[17]

A key theme common to most Anabaptist movements was the rejection of the association of church and state. They also stressed, in varying degrees and forms, adult baptism (though not necessarily by immersion), personal salvation rather than a community commitment, and having goods in common. They stressed discipleship or, as Shelley states it, they believed that "the Christian's relationship with Jesus Christ must go beyond inner experience and acceptance of doctrine. It must involve a daily walk with God, in which Christ's teaching and example shape a transformed style of life."[18] It was truly a lay movement, having very few clergy as adherents or proponents. It was violently oppressed by Lutherans and Catholics alike. And it was clearly a "free church" movement.

"There is no clear filiation between the Continental Anabaptists and the English Quakers and the American Baptists; but the Quaker rejection of war and oaths, and the Baptist insistence on adult baptism probably stem from the same traditions of creed and conduct that in Switzerland, Germany, and Holland took Anabaptist forms."[19]

The closest generic relationships to the Anabaptist movement were the Dunkers (who migrated from Germany to Pennsylvania in 1719), the Moravians (from Russia to South Dakota and Alberta), and the Amish Mennonites. The Baptists more properly derive from a wing of the English Congregational church which broke away and formed during the reign of Elizabeth I (1588-1603) concurrent with the latter part of the Reformation in Europe. Shelley points out that "in their belief in the separation of church and state the Anabaptists proved to be forerunners of practically all modern Protestants."[20]

At this same time a Counter-Reformation occurred within the Roman Catholic church. However, it was too late to stem the great tide of the Reformation.

A.D. 1648 TO 1900

In the seventeenth century, the Renaissance gave way to the Age of Reason with the great men of science, art, and philosophy—Kepler, Galileo, Newton, Shakespeare, Bacon, Rembrandt, and Descartes. Christianity witnessed the hardening of Lutheranism and Calvinism to a cold orthodoxy in a state church, and the rise of the lay movements of Quakerism and Pietism. Of particular interest in this study is the pietist movement from which many believe para-local church and independent church movements have had their impetus.

Pietism began in Germany under the leadership of Philipp Jakob Spener. It arose in protest against "the low state of the life of much of Lutheranism in its day and as a reaction against the decaying morals and religion brought to Germany by the Thirty Years' War."[21]

Pietism emphasized personal salvation, holiness of life, and study of the Bible by laymen. The early Pietists, under the scholarly influence of August Hermann Francke (Spener's successor), stimulated an early missionary movement from Halle, their center of training.

In 1722, the Moravian Brethren settled in exile on the estate of Nikolaus Ludwig Zinzendorf who had been strongly influenced by the Pietists. From this village, Herrnhut, a new missionary movement extended to the world. "Here was a new phenomenon in the expansion of Christianity, an entire community, of families as well as of the unmarried, devoted to the propagation of the faith. . . . Here was a fellowship of Christians, of laity and clergy, of men and women, marrying and rearing families, with much of the quietism of the monastery and of Pietism but with the spread of the Christian message as a major objective, not of a minority of the membership, but of the group as a whole."[22]

Another unusual aspect of the Moravians, patterned after the Pietists, was that they "never sought to bring all other Christians into their Church . . . they wished to be a leavening and transforming influence in other communions."[23]

Here we see a similar attitude to that of many para-local church societies—to help, not replace, the church. It was an unheard of emphasis to be concerned only about ministry to people without bringing them into your own fold.

The seventeenth century produced another nonchurch or para-local church phenomenon—the establishment of Protestant missionary societies which were not officially part of a church or denomination. The first of these was the Society for Promoting Christian Knowledge, founded in 1698 by Thomas Bray, rector of Sheldon and commissary in Maryland for the bishop of London. Though its members were largely from the Church of England, it was not directly under its control.

Bray also helped found the Society for the Propagation of the Gospel in Foreign Parts, in 1701. The latter was chaired by the Archbishop of Canterbury, so was closely tied to the Church of England. Others soon followed: The Society for Propagating Christian Knowledge, in 1709; the Baptist Missionary Society; the Glasgow Missionary Society; and the Scottish Missionary Society (the latter all in the 1790s).[24]

Latourette provides a perceptive summary of these efforts:

> Protestants were bringing into being new instruments
> for propagating the Christian faith. The societies which
> they were forming were without exact precedent in the

expansion of Christianity, or, indeed, in the spread of any religious faith. They were organizations, not purely of clergy, but in which laity and clergy joined. Moreover, several of them did not draw their financial support from the state or from merely a few wealthy donors, as did most of the Roman Catholic missions of the period. They appealed to a large number of donors. In some instances the initial gifts were conserved as an endowment and only the income was expended for the purposes of the society. In others the appeal was continuous. No longer did the expansion of the faith rest upon monastic orders and the state. A widening circle of clergy and laity was enlisted in the active support of missions. . . . In accord with the conviction of the priesthood of all Christians, laity shared with clergy in propagating the faith, and the financial burden for the enterprise was assumed by a growing number of the laity and by a nonmonastic clergy.[25]

These comments reflect a Protestant movement toward para-local church structures very early in their history, especially as they relate to missions. Their support and participants closely parallel para-local church groups today. The result was evangelistic outreach to many countries of the world. We presume that most of these missionary efforts were focused on some type of church planting.

One major event of the eighteenth century was the Great Awakening—a spontaneous revival in many parts of America and Europe. George Whitefield was a key evangelist and preacher during this time. This revival produced a pietistic-like individual response and subsequent godly living. John Wesley and his Methodist societies initially attempted to stay within the Church of England, rather than form another denomination. Wesley also initiated the plan of having lay preachers or helpers. After Wesley's death his followers separated from the Anglican church.

From this Great Awakening came the great American leaders of the nineteenth century, Charles G. Finney and Dwight L.

Moody. Also, many other missionary societies began to form in the United States, such as the Student Volunteer Movement for Foreign Missions, and the Young People's Society of Christian Endeavour. Many denominations grew rapidly, but the Baptists especially received impetus from this revival with its emphasis on personal piety and salvation. Puritans, Quakers, Moravians, and many others began strong missionary outreaches to the American Indians and Negroes.

A hallmark of the nineteenth century certainly must be the great movement of missions. The modern missionary movement dates back to William Carey (1761-1834) who, as a layman, had a heart for the lost of India. In the midst of church opposition he set out on his own. The result was the Baptist Missionary Society. The London Missionary Society soon caught this vision, sending out Robert Morrison to China, Robert Moffat and David Livingstone to Africa.

The London Missionary Society stated in 1795 its "fundamental principle that our design is not to send Presbyterianism, Independency, Episcopacy or any other form of church government . . . but the glorious gospel of the blessed God to the heathen."[26] Here were Christians, laity and clergy, working side by side in the common cause of the gospel. Additionally, they raised funds outside the structure of the local church.

The publication of Darwin's *Origin of Species* in 1859 began a conflict between religion and science which goes on to this day. Yet the new evangelical spirit of Protestantism was not dampened, but rather spurred on in fervent reaction.

Another key emphasis of this century was *revival*. Out of the Great Awakening came Moody, Sankey, Finney, Torrey, Wesley, Whitefield, and others who broke out of the church building pattern of both Catholic and Protestant tradition and took the gospel to the people in tents and revival halls. They had no denominational stamp, although they tended toward a branch of Calvinism without the ultra-predestination view. All people were to hear the gospel and all could respond.

Many student missionary groups developed in para-local church fashion as a response to revival and the missionary impulse.

The progenitor of these was the Student Volunteer Movement for Foreign Missions formed in the summer of 1886 under the leadership of Dwight L. Moody. It spurred a similar group in Great Britain and other Volunteer Unions of students in Europe. "It was through the Student Volunteer Movements in these various lands that a large proportion of the outstanding leaders in the world-wide spread of Protestant Christianity in the twentieth century were recruited."[27]

Latourette, in summary of the nineteenth century, makes three observations of special interest to this study:

1. The rise and prominence of women's organizations for the spread of the faith became significant in missions. In 1860 the nondenominational Women's Union Missionary Society for Heathen Lands began. Others of denominational and independent associations were formed. "The proportion of women in the missionary staffs of four of the leading American societies increased from 49 percent in 1830 to 57 percent in 1880 and to 67 percent in 1929."[28]

2. Missionary enterprise at the initiation of laymen was a new occurrence, at least on a large scale. Dwight Moody, Robert Speer (Student Volunteer Movement), and John R. Mott (YMCA) were all laymen. There were also many other laymen involved in the missionary enterprise such as William Carey and Sidney Clark of England.

3. The rapid increase of nondenominational societies spurred the modern evangelical movement. Often they were focused on specific countries, needs, or emphases. A few of these groups were:

> China Inland Mission (1865)
> The Regions Beyond Missionary Union (1878)
> Central American Mission (1890)
> Evangelical Alliance (1890)
> African Inland Mission (1895)
> Sudan Interior Mission (1901)

Other groups to meet needs other than missions were:

> The American Bible Society (1816)

American Sunday School Union (1824)
American Tract Society (1825)
Young Men's Christian Association (1844)
The Salvation Army (1865)

The Sunday school movement began as a para-local church movement. "At first it was frowned upon by many of the churches. Eventually most of the Protestant churches adopted it. . . ."[29] This acceptance came in the midnineteenth century. But it was started by Robert Raikes in 1780 to teach England's poor. An early society was formed in 1785 in London. The leadership and staff of the various Sunday school associations were predominantly lay rather than clergy. Many point to this as a prime example of the early para-local church.

In a special report, the United Presbyterian Church analyzed several of the current para-local church groups as stemming from John Darby and the early Plymouth Brethren. Once a priest in the Church of Ireland, Darby became disillusioned with its formalism and worldliness. He founded his group about 1835, drawing from Anabaptist and Brethren ideas on the continent. This later developed into the Prophecy Movement which emphasized a dispensational understanding of the Bible and premillennial eschatology. According to this report, "the Scofield Reference Bible (1910), and independent seminaries and Bible schools kept Darby's views alive and formed the seed bed from which have sprung seven current para-local church groups: Youth for Christ, Young Life, The Navigators, Campus Crusade for Christ, Fellowship of Christian Athletes, Institute in Basic Youth Conflicts and Jews for Jesus."[30]

Whether this analysis is completely accurate may be debatable, yet we do see many para-local church groups functioning strongly in an individualistic manner, concerned more for personal evangelism and private devotion than for organizational relationships. Certainly they do not spring from a clear denominational heritage except, perhaps, in reaction to denominational restrictions and slowness to change.

A.D. 1900 TO THE PRESENT

Now we enter the era of proliferation of para-local church groups. Several events dominate the background. Two world wars and two other wars of world significance (Korea and Vietnam), coupled with strife in the Middle East and other countries, make it a century of conflict with weapons of unprecedented power.

A struggle between the West and Communism consumed the minds of many from World War II to the present. The Great Depression along with other economic downtrends, interspersed with incredible prosperity in parts of the world, indelibly affected the mindset of many in America. The advent of nuclear arms and missiles put the world on the edge of fear.

World War I dealt a near death blow to the liberal notion of the goodness of man and a utopia of world peace.

America, untouched physically by the wars and generally boiling with vigor, prominence, and prosperity, became the seed bed for religious renewal. The Fundamentalist-Modernist controversy of the 1930s so occupied the minds of many churchmen that other issues faded into obscurity. Many new denominations resulted from the subsequent splits in old-line denominations. As the battle lines were drawn, both sides became more inflexible. Fundamental Christianity withdrew into a defensive position. The thirties and forties were a time of evangelical entrenchment, many becoming isolationist and ineffective in their outreach. During this period a number of new para-local church societies began, partially in frustration with the infighting and entrenchment, and partially to meet needs they saw as unmet by the organized church.

This period saw the advance of radio and television, air transportation, mass communication, accelerated publication of books and other materials, all of which influenced people in new ways. Charles Fuller's "The Old Fashioned Revival Hour" paved the way for thousands of radio preachers and subsequent television preachers. Following in the Moody revivalist tradition, Billy Graham brought in a new era of mass evangelism. For thirty-five years, Graham has been a major religious force in America. Though controversial to some, Graham again brought Christianity and evangelism outside the walls of the church building, and reached the man on the street in a manner unprecedented in history.

Following World War II, thousands of soldiers returned home to give their lives to reach a world into which war had thrust them and had opened their eyes to its needs. They went to colleges, Bible schools, and seminaries, then flooded back to Asia, China, and Europe—many in new interdenominational para-local church mission agencies. Others stayed home and helped form new groups to reach people in the United States.

"A wave of Christian organizations rolled across the U.S. at the end of World War II. Energetic, visionary young men boarded DC-3s and criss-crossed continents. With evangelistic zeal and a sense of America's new leadership, they mounted a sort of spiritual Marshall Plan. They held large meetings, printed literature, made movies and sought out the needy and displaced peoples in former theatres of war."[31]

In the fifties, more and more laymen began to seek ministries of a specialist nature outside the traditional bounds of the church, though most remained in their local congregations. In the early years (thirties and forties) many were disillusioned and impatient with the entrenched evangelical church establishment. Few wanted to replace it, but simply to supplement and stimulate it. Conflict was inevitable, as it was historically with any movement that crossed the boundaries or prerogatives of the traditional church structure.

Diversity has always been a characteristic of the American Protestant church. No less in the para-local church movement do we find diversity. In fact, its diversity is almost part of its genesis. Whereas the church is primarily generalist in its ministry, the para-local church societies are narrowly specialist. Their plethora of specializations include personal and small group evangelism, church planting, mass evangelism, literature distribution, broadcasting, theological education, medicine, agriculture, relief, aviation, camping, communications, discipleship, fund raising, management consulting, orphanages, translation, youth ministries, and a host of others. Some of these ministries can and are being done by denominational structures, but rarely do they do them all.

In our age of specialization, the Christian ministry is both benefited and complicated by the specialization of efforts.

In this same period of growth for the para-local church, the
evangelical church has also made great forward strides as it has
grown in numbers and in stature as a strong religious force in
America. The para-local church has by no means replaced the local
congregation—they have both benefited from each other. At the
same time, liberal churches are shrinking and losing their effectiveness and respect.

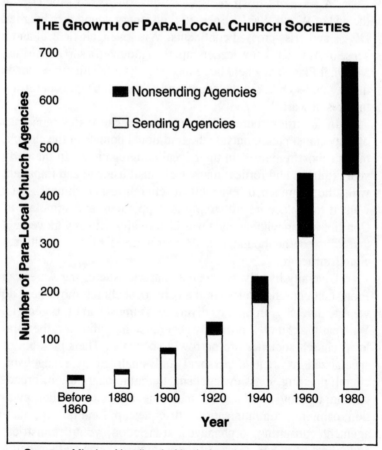

Source: *Mission Handbook: North American Protestant Ministries
Overseas,* 12th ed. (Monrovia, Calif.: MARC, 1979), pp. 52-53.

The sixties and seventies have precipitated a great upsurge in para-local church societies of every kind.

From this chart we see the almost exponential growth of para-local church societies. This chart is both incomplete and conservative. It shows only North American mission agencies with overseas ministries. The growth is actually much greater.

HISTORICAL SUMMARY AND OBSERVATIONS

The above history is necessarily brief and narrow, merely tracing history with an eye for special threads that relate to our topic. There are many other significant threads of history—the doctrine of salvation, the history of missions, the view of Scripture, the structure of the local congregation, and so on. In looking for one aspect, it is possible to ignore or overlook others. However, in viewing church history since the first century, a number of observations can be made that will help us understand the reasons for the proliferation of para-local church organizations.

1. Conflict and division have been dishearteningly present in every century up to the present day. Both internal and external conflict have been the norm.

2. Almost every significant change in structure or practice, especially after the third century, was resisted by the established church structure. Peaceful internal reform was rare, if not nonexistent.

3. After every new movement, the tendency was toward institutionalization of the precepts and structure, resulting in rigidity and inflexibility.

4. Most "evangelical" movements were in the minority until the Reformation. God always seemed to work through a few to keep the true gospel message extant.

5. Doctrine, structure, and authority have always been a major point of conflict. Anything outside the existing structure or authority line was considered illegitimate or unbiblical.

6. Most changes or movements began as reforms rather than secessions.

7. Many movements for change were heretical and unbibli-

cal. Most were short-lived. Others were absorbed by the Roman Catholic church and led to its decay. Some remain in it today.

8. When change was attempted, one of three things resulted: the church responded and allowed reform, the movement was crushed and disappeared, or it caused a permanent separation from the parent body.

9. Many of the movements had political and social as well as spiritual issues at stake. The changes often were deeply influenced by the culture and the environment of the time.

10. "Right" did not always win out, nor was survival a mark of God's blessing. Each movement must be examined in the light of Scripture, not in light of its continuing existence.

11. God cannot be put in a box. He will use diverse methods, structures, and people to accomplish his work in the world. Whether it be unorthodox or unprecedented, through clergy or laity, God will do according to his pleasure and purpose, not according to our limited view of how he "ought" to work.

ANALYSIS OF PROLIFERATION, 1960 TO THE PRESENT

Even if we admit to the validity of para-local church groups, the great increase in numbers of groups over the past twenty years causes us to look for reasons for the sudden expansion. As I have viewed the movements from both sides of the fence, certain fundamental reasons come to the surface.

1. The churches' inability to use laymen and women in full-time capacities. Imagine a gifted layman in the church, in his midthirties, experienced in ministry skills and solid in his knowledge of the Scriptures. He decides that God is calling him into a full-time ministry other than the pastorate. As he shares this desire with his pastor, the usual reply is, "That's great. I'm fully supportive of your desire. Where do you plan to go to seminary?"

The layman shares that he really did not intend to go to seminary, but wants to join the church staff or at least be sponsored by the church. He discovers that this simply is not done. After more frustration and prayer, he decides to begin his own ministry by establishing a new para-local church organization.

Vast numbers of para-local church staff are laymen or women who have not had recognized formal training.

> As missions, the parachurch groups have been able to use talent that would never be used in a fulltime function in regular churches. Inter-Varsity, Navigators, Faith at Work and other groups have some gifted staffs who would never be ordained into the formal ministry of churches. Some of them are women—intelligent, people oriented, good Bible students—but how many churches have a "position" for a woman in their paid ministry? The independent agencies have created such a structure.[32]

Until the local church learns to integrate gifted lay people into their ministries on a full-time basis and to send them out as missionaries, they will continue to flood to para-local church agencies or form their own. In the local church, we are in danger of institutionalizing the preparation for ministry to our own hurt.

2. An independent spirit. It is one thing to have *some* specialist organizations, but the great proliferation does raise some questions about actual need. Some form their own organization because of an independent spirit that prevents them from working harmoniously in another group or a local church. Many organizations have been spawned from existing organizations. It is likely that all are not really necessary or fruitful. Yet some people cannot seem to work under the authority of another. They have to be completely independent, and they bow to no authority but their own. Even though many small organizations have boards of directors, rarely is the principal worker under their authority in practice.

3. The United States tax laws. Beginning one's own organization today is almost as easy as opening a bank account. Under our tax laws a nonprofit corporation can be established for almost any purpose. A board of directors, a tax-exempt number for receipting purposes, and a new organization is in business. Changing tax laws and a tightening economy could have a drastic effect on para-local church groups, especially the smaller ones.

The seminary and Bible school, while offering excellent

training, can become an institutionalized bottleneck if we insist that they remain the primary source of fulltime ministry candidates.

4. The individualism of our age and the American frontier spirit. Individualism is a primary virtue of the American way of life. Different, new, creative, and personal are words that intrigue the American individualist. J. Alan Youngren describes it as the frontier spirit:

> Four characteristics of the frontier mind we Americans inherit still serve to increase our enthusiasm for the parachurch alternative: (1) less respect for tradition and traditional social structures; (2) communalism—an attitude favoring the autonomy of one's own community or group; (3) self-reliance and an independent spirit; (4) infatuation with almost anything new.[33]

5. The unmet needs. There are areas of legitimate need which the church, and particularly a single local congregation, would not or cannot meet. The local church simply does not penetrate some areas with the gospel. Mission sending agencies have spurred outreach to lands untouched by the church. Some para-local church groups do serve the local congregation significantly; others specialize to fulfill particular needs. History aptly demonstrates that there have always been gaps the organized church has not even attempted to fill.

6. God's initiative. Throughout history we see God intervening in the affairs of the church with new structures and methods. God has sovereignly called and used many para-local church structures throughout history to jolt the established church, to reform it, and to reach out in unique ways to penetrate unreached peoples.

But the questions still remain. Has God called all para-local church groups into being? Are they all fulfilling a need in the kingdom of God? We must also ask another threatening question. Has God called all local congregations and denominations into being?

Chapter 2, Notes

1. Stephen Board, "The Great Evangelical Power Shift," *Eternity,* June 1979, p. 17.

2. *The World Christian Encyclopedia* (New York: Oxford University Press, 1982).

3. Board, "Power Shift," p. 17.

4. Kenneth Scott Latourette, *A History of the Expansion of Christianity,* vol. 1: *The First Five Centuries* (Grand Rapids: Zondervan Publishing House, 1970), pp. 328-34.

5. Harold Cook, "Who Really Sent the First Missionaries?" *Evangelical Missions Quarterly* 12 (1975): 233-39.

6. Bruce L. Shelley, *Church History in Plain Language* (Waco, Tex.: Word Books, 1982), p. 85.

7. Shelley, *Church History,* p. 91.

8. Shelley, *Church History,* pp. 143-44.

9. Henry Bettenson, *The Early Christian Fathers* (London: Oxford University Press, 1956), p. 370.

10. Shelley, *Church History,* p. 185.

11. Will Durant, *The Story of Civilization,* vol. 4: *The Age of Faith* (New York: Simon and Schuster, 1950), p. 769.

12. Durant, *Age of Faith,* p. 769.

13. Durant, *Age of Faith,* p. 770.

14. Shelley, *Church History,* p. 227.

15. Kenneth Scott Latourette, *A History of the Expansion of Christianity,* vol. 2: *The Thousand Years of Uncertainty* (Grand Rapids: Zondervan Publishing House, 1970), pp. 16, 18.

16. Will Durant, *The Story of Civilization,* vol. 6: *The Reformation* (New York: Simon and Schuster, 1957), p. 362.

17. Kenneth Scott Latourette, *A History of the Expansion of Christianity,* vol. 3: *Three Centuries of Advance* (Grand Rapids: Zondervan Publishing House, 1970), pp. 436-37.

18. Shelley, *Church History,* p. 271.

19. Durant, *Reformation,* pp. 401-2

20. Shelley, *Church History,* p. 266.

21. Latourette, *Three Centuries,* p. 14.

22. Latourette, *Three Centuries,* p. 47.

23. Latourette, *Three Centuries,* p. 48.

24. Latourette, *Three Centuries,* pp. 49-50.

25. Latourette, *Three Centuries,* pp. 50-51.

26. Shelley, *Church History,* p. 408.

27. Kenneth Scott Latourette, *A History of the Expansion of Christianity,* vol. 4: *The Great Century: In Europe and the United States of America* (Grand Rapids: Zondervan Publishing House, 1970), p. 98.

28. Latourette, *Great Century*, p. 98.

29. Latourette, *Great Century*, p. 376.

30. United Presbyterian Church in the USA, "Para-Church Groups: A Report on Current Religious Movements," New York, n.d., pp. 17-18.

31. Ron Wilson, "Para-Church: Becoming Part of the Body," *Christianity Today*, Sept. 19, 1980, pp. 18-20.

32. Board, "Power Shift," p. 21.

33. J. Alan Youngren, "Parachurch Proliferation: The Frontier Spirit Caught in Traffic," *Christianity Today*, Nov. 6, 1981, p. 39.

"Now the Bereans were of more noble character than the Thessalonians, for they received the message with great eagerness and examined the Scriptures every day to see if what Paul said was true."
Acts 17:11

Chapter 3

A Theological Perspective

*T*heology rarely resolves conflict since most conflict in and among churches is seldom truly theological. Consequently, embarking upon a theological examination of local church and para-local church issues becomes almost futile, since so many people react strictly from their own theological training or from a pragmatic position based on experience. As we consider the validity of the para-local church, we first must determine what we will accept as our authority. Our choices are:

1. Scripture alone
2. Scripture and church history
3. Scripture, church history, and tradition
4. Scripture, church history, tradition, and current human authority (i.e., a pope)

Most people of evangelical and conservative theological persuasion would accept only the first option—the Scriptures. However, some Protestant evangelicals would also place some emphasis on a combination of options 2 and 3. They have a strong respect for traditions yet admit the primacy of Scripture.

It is my view that history and tradition must always be evaluated in light of Scripture. History shows how various godly men of the past interpreted the Scriptures and applied them to their culture, but it does not tell us what Scripture necessarily teaches.

But first we need a more detailed description of para-local church structures.

THE SPECTRUM OF PARA-LOCAL CHURCH STRUCTURES

By our definition of a para-local church (p. 19), *we must recognize every ministry structure other than a local congregation as a para-local church structure.* In some theological traditions a denomination is viewed as the local church or simply the church. It is true that some structures are more closely related to the local congregation than others. But where do we draw the line?

Denominational structures, associational structures, seminaries, Bible schools, denominational mission agencies, independent mission agencies, as well as a multitude of relief, translation, evangelistic, discipleship, church service, and other specialist agencies are all para-local church structures.

We can view these para-local church structures in relationship to local congregations.[1] The chart on the following page shows the categories of para-local church groups and their level of independence from local congregations.

Some people may not consider some of these structures to be para-local churches if they are denominationally controlled, or if they directly supply churches or even plant churches. But that is simply convenience of definition. Theologically, each person draws the line somewhere in that spectrum in determining the legitimacy of an agency.

In my survey, some considered any structure controlled by a local congregation or groups of local congregations as part of the local church. But this leads to confusion. Does this mean pastors must be on the board of directors? Must there be a board member from each local church? Can laymen serve on the board? Can they be from different denominations or associations? As you can see, drawing the line where local church structure ends and where para-local church structure begins is no easy task. Usually the distinction becomes pragmatic, not theological.

PARA-LOCAL CHURCH STRUCTURES IN RELATIONSHIP TO LOCAL CONGREGATIONS

The Local Congregation

Direct
- Denominational Structures
- Associational Structures

Church Supplying
- Denominational Seminaries
- Independent Seminaries
- Christian Schools (College and below)

Church Planting
- Denominational Mission Agencies
- Independent Mission Agencies

Church Renewal and Service
- Denominational Evangelists
- Interdenominational Evangelists
- Church Service Organizations

Specialist
- Independent Evangelism/Discipling Agencies
- Specially Focused Agencies (Jews, Youth, etc.)
- Publishing Houses
- Hospitals and Relief Agencies

Increasing Independence from Local Congregations

SIX THEOLOGICAL PERSPECTIVES

In evangelical Christianity today, we can identify six theological views regarding the para-local church. (In later discussions, we will refer to these different perspectives by means of a descriptive word or phrase.)

1. Local church only. This view judges any structure outside the local congregation as illegitimate. All mission sending or other efforts must be under the direct authority of a local congregation. Any outreach or mission effort must result in church planting.

2. *Temporary legitimacy*. This view believes that the local church is God's primary agency for ministry in the world. However, para-local church structures have been raised up for a *temporary* corrective influence on the local church. When the church begins meeting the need as it should, para-local church structures should disappear.

3. *Two-structures*. This view has been expounded strongly by Ralph Winter[2] and many of the church growth writers. Winter describes the local and mobile (modality and sodality) as two distinct biblical structures in God's plan. The local congregation meets the growth needs of a body of believers. The mobile function is the mission outreach of evangelizing and discipling in the world.

4. *Church planting*. This position gives legitimacy to para-local church societies as long as their goal is church planting. It is insufficient to simply perform a part of the function of a church, such as evangelism, if a direct result is not integration into an existing congregation or planting a new one.

5. *Dual legitimacy*. Dual legitimacy indicates that both the local congregation and para-local church are legitimate expressions of God working in the body of Christ. It permits varied kinds of structures both in missions and local expressions. Since all are part of the broader body of Christ, individual believers, though part of a local congregation, express their ministry to the world in a variety of semi-autonomous structures. This differs from the two-structures view in that it does not require the two-structures analysis, and would allow for nonmobile para-local church agencies (a rescue mission, a local businessmen's outreach, a seminary) and nonmissionary specialists.

6. *Anti-institutional*. This view looks upon the church in its institutions, organizations, and buildings as ineffective and unnecessary. It seeks nearly total freedom in individual expression with resistance to authority from either a local or para-local church.

Having stated six possible ways of viewing the local church and its relationship to para-local church societies or structures, we need to examine more carefully the scriptural teaching on the local church.

WHAT IS THE LOCAL CHURCH?

Many fine books have been written attempting to answer this very question. Controversy raged over the centuries and resulted in the 20,800 denominational expressions existing today. The unity of the body of Ephesians 4:1-6 and other passages appears to be an almost unattainable goal. Even if we granted complete autonomy to local congregations, each would approve only a small segment of the other local congregations depending on similarities in doctrine and practice.

This situation led one pastor to remark to another, "I believe the only people who really have biblical churches are you and me. And sometimes I wonder about you!" This variation on an old joke expresses our inability to agree in the body of Christ.

The beginning of the body of Christ, the church, is viewed in two ways. Reformed or covenant theologians believe the church dates back to God's covenant with Abraham, the body of Christ being an extension of Israel. Others believe the church was initiated at Pentecost. In either case, today's church must be consistent with the New Testament teaching about concept and structure.

Knowing that no study, brief or exhaustive, will satisfy all readers, let us consider the most common elements concerning the nature of the local church.

First, *any* local congregation is an admixture of believers and unbelievers. No matter how carefully prospective members are interviewed, some unsaved people will join our churches. They are religious, but not saved. Some join simply out of ignorance or a misunderstanding of the gospel message. Others join a church, even deceptively, to maintain family unity. We see the presence of unbelievers in the church in New Testament times with the problems caused by false prophets and false teachers (*see* 2 Peter 2:1-3; 2 Timothy 3:1-9; 4:3-4).

Second, we know that membership in a local congregation is not requisite for salvation. "For it is by grace you have been saved through faith—and this not from yourselves, it is the gift of God" (Ephesians 2:8). Baptism, communion, and good works are acts of obedience for the believer, not the instruments of salvation.

Third, we know there are believers who are not part of a local congregation. They may be new believers in isolation. They may be in a situation, such as imprisonment or persecution, where no viable local fellowship exists. They may have left a local church that was not evangelical and are seeking one that is.

God knows those who are his own and are part of the universal church, the body of Christ.

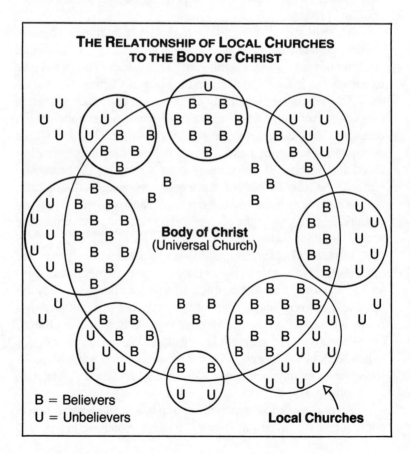

THE RELATIONSHIP OF LOCAL CHURCHES TO THE BODY OF CHRIST

Body of Christ (Universal Church)

B = Believers
U = Unbelievers

Local Churches

This brings us to a bit of tension between the concept of the universal church and the local church. At one extreme, the universal church can become an excuse for not being related to the local congregation. At the other extreme is the idea that the universal church is made up *only* of those who are members of a local church. The worst case, which becomes heretical, is the view that one must be a part of *a particular local church* to be a part of the body of Christ. Both the universal church and the local church are clearly taught in Scripture.

THE NEW TESTAMENT DOCTRINE OF THE UNIVERSAL CHURCH

The Greek word *ekklesia,* like many words in the New Testament, is a common word that was adapted and redefined by its special usage by the New Testament writers. *Ekklesia* simply means an assembly, such as the legal assembly referred to in Acts 19:39-41. In the Septuagint (Greek translation of the Old Testament), it is used many times to refer to the congregation or assembly of Israel.

In Earl Radmacher's book, *What the Church Is All About,* he classifies every New Testament use of *ekklesia.* Radmacher notes two basic uses: *technical* (meaning the local assembly or church) and *metaphorical* (meaning the universal church or body of Christ). It is interesting that the local church is not mentioned one time in the entire epistle of Ephesians, the epistle we often turn to for teaching on the church. In every case in Ephesians, *ekklesia* refers to the universal church.

> "And God . . . appointed him [Christ] to be head over everything for the church, which is his body . . ." (1:22-23).

> ". . . through the church, the manifold wisdom of God should be made known to the rulers and authorities in the heavenly realms . . ." (3:10).

> ". . . to him be glory in the church and in Christ Jesus throughout all generations . . ." (3:21).

> ". . . Christ is the head of the church, his body, of which he is the Savior" (5:23).

"Now as the church submits to Christ . . ." (5:24).

". . . just as Christ loved the church . . ." (5:25).

". . . to present her to himself as a radiant church . . . holy and blameless" (5:27).

"After all, no one ever hated his own body, but he feeds and cares for it, just as Christ does the church—for we are members of his body" (5:29-30).

"This is a profound mystery—but I am talking about Christ and the church" (5:32).

Radmacher also classifies *ekklesia* in Matthew 16:18 ("I will build my church"), Colossians 1:18 ("he is the head of the body, the church"), and Hebrews 12:23 ("to the church of the firstborn") as the church universal. He summarizes,

> The doctrine of the universal church arises out of an inductive study and systemization of the metaphorical usages of *ekklesia* in the New Testament. When the Apostle Paul comes to the metaphorical use of the *ekklesia* (predominantly in Ephesians and Colossians), he conceives of an entire world of individual Christians immediately related to Christ apart from local *ekklesiai*, and he terms them simply the (only) *ekklesia*. Thus, the concept of the physical assembly gives way to the spiritual assembly.[3]

The existence of the universal church can also be supported by other metaphorical expressions in the New Testament. In Ephesians 2, Paul teaches that believing Jews and Gentiles are now one in Christ. "Consequently, you are no longer foreigners and aliens, but fellow citizens with God's people and members of God's household, built on the foundation of the apostles and prophets, with Christ Jesus himself as the chief cornerstone. In him the whole building is joined together and rises to become a holy temple in the Lord. And in him you too are being built together to become a dwelling in which God lives by his Spirit" (vv. 19-22). "God's people" are all believers, and "God's household," the "whole building," and "a holy temple" are all expressions of the body of Christ. Note that these descriptions are not plural but singular, denoting one. The plural would be required to depict multiple local churches.

The term "body" is used in several other places in Ephesians.

"The Gentiles . . . members together of one body" (3:6).

"There is one body" (4:4).

"It was he who gave some . . . so that the body of Christ may be built up" (4:11-12).

"From him [Christ] the whole body, joined and held together by every supporting ligament, grows and builds itself up in love, as each part does its work" (4:16).

In addition, metaphors other than the body of Christ are used for the universal church. It is a building (1 Peter 2:5), a priesthood (1 Peter 2:5, 9), a flock (1 Peter 5:21), and branches of a vine (John 15:5).

We have established, at least in summary form, the New Testament doctrine of the universal church. Unfortunately, this doctrine has been misapplied and carried to some unfavorable extremes. One of those extremes is the growth of what Radmacher calls "nonreciprocal interdenominational groups."

Another unhappy result of an inaccurate application of this doctrine is the appearance of numerous interdenominational organizations, many of which are necessary and good, working through local churches and supplementing their ministry; but some of these organizations are usurping the responsibilities and functions that God intended for the local church to perform. Many of these groups began as a result of the failure of the local church in certain areas. They were supported by people of vision within the local churches. Some of these groups became nonreciprocal in that while they received their support from the local churches, they themselves failed to work together with the local churches. As a result, oftentimes there is needless duplication of ministries. Furthermore, the support of these organizations interferes with the necessary financial backing for the local church, necessitates the redirecting of valuable time that should be spent in Christian service through the local church, and destroys a proper loyalty to the local church.[4]

The existence of the universal church does not replace the validity and necessity of the local congregation. The local congregation is an expresson of the universal church. Some who take the doctrine of the universal church to an unfavorable extreme try to negate the need for a local church. "Such a de-emphasis of the local church displays ignorance of the biblical teaching that repeatedly attributes the existence of the local churches to the Godhead (cf. 1 Cor. 11:16; Gal. 1:22; 1 Thess. 2:14; 2 Thess. 1:4; etc.)."[5]

The New Testament Doctrine of the Local Church

But where do we see the local church in Scripture? We see it in many places from Acts through Revelation. In fact, *ekklesia* is used in its technical sense, referring to the local congregation, in 90 out of its 114 occurrences in the New Testament.[6] Though referred to frequently, it is not as carefully defined as we might like. The local church is simply the physical, outward expression of the universal church. Paul addressed several of his epistles to specific local churches ("To the church of the Thessalonians . . .", 1 and 2 Thessalonians 1:1; also 1 Corinthians 1:2; 2 Corinthians 1:1). In Galatians 1:2 we find, "To the churches [note the plural] in Galatia." In Revelation 1:11, John was instructed to write to "the seven churches." Paul referred not just to specific churches, but to many local churches in many places when he wrote, "He [Timothy] will remind you of my way of life in Christ Jesus, which agrees with what I teach everywhere in every church" (1 Corinthians 4:17).

Yet there are many things we do not know about these local assemblies. Take, for instance, the church in Corinth.

- Was it one church or many?
- If many, were they related?

- Was there a central authority over them?
- Were they related to local churches in any other city?
- Was there a central place of worship?

Scripture does not answer these questions as completely as we would like. From the scriptural data, or lack thereof, we can ascertain several things. There were several household churches in most of the cities (Romans 16:5, "Greet also the church that meets at their house." Also Colossians 4:15; Philemon 2). We have no record of a building or larger meeting place in any city. We have no data on how these smaller churches related to each other. There may have been some relationship between the elders (Acts 20:17, ". . . Paul sent to Ephesus for the elders of the church"). The plural use of "elders" and singular use of "church" could indicate a unified Ephesian church, but the data is scant. We note that there was communication between the churches in various cities, but we do not see any central authority over them. The Jerusalem church exerted some influence but did not exercise direct authority.

We do see what the church is *not*. It is not a building (the church on the corner of 5th and Main), but a group of people. The church is not a particular set of weekly meetings or order of service. The church is not pure in the sense of having no unsaved in it.

How then do we identify the local church? It is fundamentally a local community of believers of diverse age and socioeconomic strata who band together under a designated leadership structure for fellowship, teaching, worship, and outreach to the lost. It is not the building or the organizational structure.

THE STRUCTURE OF THE LOCAL CHURCH

As we examine the New Testament, we find surprisingly few details about local congregational structure, how often the church should assemble, order of service, or even the specific functions of elders or deacons. We do see the specific *qualifications* of elders and deacons in 1 Timothy 3 and Titus 1, but no comprehensive job descriptions. Even the "shepherd" instructions of 1 Peter 5 present only an implied or allegorical job description.

We get illustrative glimpses, but not directives. Except for the matter of church discipline, we see even less of how the church directs individual activities of its members. Here is a summary of what we do know with certainty.

1. The church met on the first day of the week (Acts 20:7). Some feel this is the designated day because of the resurrection. Others feel it is the "new sabbath." It may well have been simply a practical time (perhaps even at night) because of the Jewish sabbath. We cannot mandate or limit the congregational meeting to only Sunday. Certainly it became tradition and unfortunately carried with it some of the sabbath restrictions. A minimum of a weekly meeting is taught and practiced in the New Testament.

2. They celebrated the Lord's supper (1 Corinthians 11:17-34). There is, however, no restriction on who serves it, how it is done, or how often. There is also no restriction on whether it is a function of the entire church or of just a few believers. All of these restrictions came from our tradition and practice, not Scripture. The concept of pressed wafers, plastic cups, and organ music is form, not scriptural function.

3. They practiced exhortation, teaching, singing, and prayer (Hebrews 10:24-25; Ephesians 4:11-13; 1 Timothy 4:13; Colossians 3:16). How long the service lasted, we do not know (on one occasion, Paul preached for hours—Acts 20:7). As indicated in 1 Corinthians 14:40, there was to be order and orderliness; but what the order was we do not know.

4. Elders and deacons were selected and filled specific offices (1 Timothy 3:1; Titus 1:5). We do not know how many of each there were, nor do we know their interrelationships (i.e., chief elder, authority of one elder over another, and so on). How they were selected is not mandated. In Titus (1:5) and Acts (14:23), they were appointed. From 1 Timothy 5:17 we see that they were to rule in some fashion or to exercise authority. In James 5:14 they prayed for the sick.

5. The local church was to care for widows (1 Timothy 5:1-16). It is unusual today for this to be a stated function of any church, much less a practice. But it is a specific scriptural injunction.

6. *Baptism was practiced.* However, we have little record after the beginning of Acts that it was an exclusive function of the church. Philip, a layman, was not in a church meeting when he baptized the Ethiopian (Acts 8:38). The Philippian jailer and his family were baptized at night, presumably in his own house (Acts 16:33).

These are significant functions which should be—and are— practiced in our local congregations today. But does it bother you that little is recorded about the organization and order of these functions? Does it shake your confidence in the traditions and forms your church body practices? It should, if you believe those forms have a solid biblical basis. But it should not, if you realize that we have great freedom in organizing the functions in our local churches today.

Here we encounter the important concept of *form* and *function.* We know from Scripture several *functions* of a local church and many functions of individual believers. But the *form* of these functions is not carefully spelled out in the Scriptures. And there is a good reason. This gives great freedom for cultural adaptation of the forms to fit and aid the functions. A church with an altar, pews, and an 11:00 A.M. service may not be practical or possible in many parts of the world.

Francis Schaeffer states this point well:

> It is my thesis that as we cannot bind men morally except where the Scripture clearly commands (beyond that we can only give advice), similarly *anything the New Testament does not command concerning church form is a freedom to be exercised under the leadership of the Holy Spirit for that particular time and place.* In other words, the New Testament sets boundary conditions, but within these boundary conditions there is much freedom to meet the changes that arise both in different places and different times. . . .[7]

It seems clear to me that the opposite cannot be

held—namely, that only that which is commanded is allowed. If this were the case, then, for example, to have
a church building would be wrong and so would having
church bells or a pulpit, using books for singing, following any specific order of service, standing to sing,
and many other like things. If consistently held in practice, I doubt if any church could function or worship.[8]

This statement is highly perceptive and accurate. We are so
easily detoured by the details of form that we lose sight of the function. Two services on Sunday, Sunday school, and a midweek
prayer meeting are fine traditions, but are simply man's invention
to perform needed functions. Let us not use them as law.

One issue of structure which causes occasional controversy is
the concept of church membership in the way we practice it today,
since believers were identified not by having their names on the
church roll, but by their association and involvement with a local
church. Certainly they were recognized as church members or else
they could not have been disciplined or expelled.

In our age of "secular" church and of the proliferation of
churches, membership provides a convenient way to identify a
two-way commitment between an individual and the local body.
Churches that have no formal membership have ways of identify-
ing the "real" members as they consider them for offices and other
tasks. Again, we use membership as part of a smooth-functioning
local church.

As we come to the end of this discussion of structure, it
would be helpful to see the great spectrum of structures in local
churches today. The chart on the following page shows the relationship between local church structure and centralized authority.

As we view this great variation in the structures of various
local churches, we can become confused about what is biblical.
Even within evangelical circles there is wide variation. Our previous discussion of the structure of a local church revealed the considerable freedom of form that may be used. Most structures and
forms, even in "unstructured" local congregations, are a result of

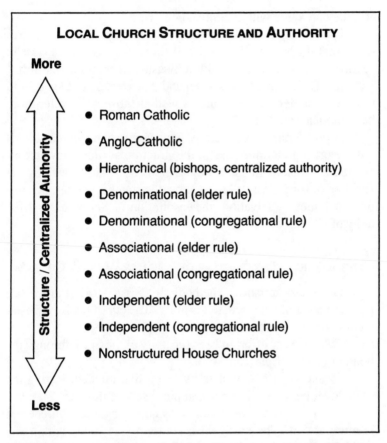

tradition or current cultural choice. But they are not therefore unbiblical.

We exercise freedom of form to determine the frequency of our meetings, the order of service, the length of the preaching, the music, the youth groups, the prayer meetings, and the Sunday schools. We can biblically express this freedom as long as the forms fulfill the biblical function.

We cannot mandate our forms for everyone, or treat them as sacred. Schaeffer states, *"The central fact is that the early concept of the church had no connection with a church building."* [9] Buildings are not wrong or unbiblical. Excesses in their architecture may raise financial questions, but as a form meeting a need in our society, they are quite within biblical bounds.

I personally like to know what comes next in a service, and to know that if I go at 9:45 A.M. I will find a Sunday school class in session. I am comfortable with a measure of tradition and form. But I must admit that I cannot demand it just because I like it. Both those who prefer less structure as well as those who prefer more have biblical freedom.

A proliferation of structure, however, may result in a doctrinal change in function. That is, the structure or ritual may be considered efficacious in some way. This is not what I mean by the freedom of form. We still must keep doctrinally clear on such important issues as salvation, the inspiration of Scripture, and the deity of Christ.

THEOLOGICAL PERSPECTIVE ON THE PARA-LOCAL CHURCH

One characteristic of the body of Christ, local or universal, that we have not yet discussed is unity. The cry of the New Testament is for unity in the body.

"Make every effort to keep the unity of the Spirit through the bond of peace" (Ephesians 4:3).

"Make my joy complete by being like-minded, having the same love, being one in spirit and purpose" (Philippians 2:2).

Where is that peace and unity in and among local churches? It is often absent. The evangelical church today fights within and without. Regularly we hear of splits and schisms in the best of churches. People leave and start another church nearby. Before long, even these churches are divided. Too seldom do we see unity between one local church and another—especially if they are not of the same denomination or association. The key characteristics of witness to the world—love and unity—simply are not present in so many fellowships. Why not?

We are too ingrown and concerned about our own things. We need to apply Philippians 2:4 to our local churches, "Each of you should look not only to your own interests, but also to the interests of others." We seemingly cannot get along with each other. The frontier spirit of America applies to local churches as well as to individuals. I do not at all advocate an indiscriminate ecumenical stance. But surely, other churches are also being used by God, are they not? Our inability to cooperate with others in the body of Christ and our isolationist attitude is a great blot on the witness of the church in the world.

God so graciously works through the local church. And if we propose that God's primary method of ministry to believers and the world is the local church, we must ask a hard question: Which church?

Which church in *your* neighborhood is the one God uses? Is it the Baptist, the other Baptist, the Presbyterian, the Pentecostal, the Free Church, the Covenant church, or the Lutheran church? Do we simply say that God will use *any* local church? Within a five mile radius of my home there are over thirty churches. Which one is the church of my city? Can we say that each has its purpose in God's plan? Even among those we class as conservative or evangelical, which one is God using? I personally subscribe to the autonomy of local congregations. But were the various local congregations in Rome unrelated to one another? I think not. Were they isolated from each other and essentially competitors? Again, I think not. We must practice a broader view of the body of Christ while still focusing on our particular calling and task.

Another issue to consider: How much authority does a local church exert over its members? The reason for this question is the concept that all ministry must be under the authority of a local congregation rather than a para-local church structure. Let me illustrate with the following situations, I hope not oversimplified.

Suppose I work for the Boeing Company in Seattle. I decide to start a Bible study at work. Two other Christians and I, all from different churches, decide to lead it together and to invite several non-Christians to join us. Under whose authority is my ministry in that study? Which local church should claim it as "their" outreach?

In a neighborhood, two couples decide to have an outreach to non-Christians. The couples go to different churches, yet share the leadership of the study. Under whose authority is that study? Is it illegitimate to work in this way with a couple from another church because there is no longer a clear line of authority? If several people in the study come to Christ, to whose church should they go?

I believe we could rejoice in both Bible studies. Perhaps the most ultraseparatistic Christians would frown on such activities, but they would have to admit that people are being reached for Christ and are studying the Bible. But these ministries are not under the authority of a local church. In a technical sense, both studies are para-local church structures.

Before we extend such an example to the large para-local church societies, we need to consider the function and responsibilities of the individual believer in a local congregation. Earlier, I pointed out the critical issue of unity. There is another issue which is critical both doctrinally and practically. It is the priesthood of the believer.

"You also, like living stones, are being built into a spiritual house to be a holy priesthood, offering spiritual sacrifices acceptable to God through Jesus Christ. . . . But you are a chosen people, a royal priesthood, a holy nation, a people belonging to God . . ." (1 Peter 2:5, 9).

"And [he] has made us to be a kingdom and priests to serve his God and Father . . ." (Revelation 1:6).

Under the new covenant, the believer has direct access and individual responsibility to God without the intercession of an earthly priest. This priesthood brings a new freedom for the believer, both in worship and in service. It is the cornerstone of the ministry of every believer. Thus the believer as an individual and the believer in fellowship with other believers has personal responsibility to obey God's commands about evangelism, discipleship, serving others, helping the poor, and so on.

He is also personally responsible to exercise his gifts. The spiritual gifts of believers are given for the building up of the entire body of Christ, not just the local church. God certainly uses these gifts in the local congregation, but they are not the property of that congregation. They belong to the whole body.

> The body is a unit, though it is made up of many
> parts; and though all its parts are many, they form one

body. So it is with Christ. For we were all baptized by one Spirit into one body—whether Jews or Greeks, slave or free—and we were all given the one Spirit to drink. . . .

Now you are the body of Christ, and each one of you is a part of it. And in the church [*ekklesia*, metaphorical usage, universal church] God has appointed first of all apostles, second prophets, third teachers, then workers of miracles, also those having gifts of healing, those able to help others, those with gifts of administration and those speaking in different kinds of tongues (1 Corinthians 12:12-13, 27-28).

When viewing the ministry in the entire body of Christ, I see no restriction on a structured ministry not under the direct control of a local church or denomination. The members of a local church are not restrained from forming other associations for spiritual purposes. Para-local church structures, made up of individual believers around a common purpose, are as much a part of the universal church as any local congregation. On the other hand, para-local church organizations also cannot claim that a particular believer must minister exclusively under the auspices of their organization. The key question for local church and para-local church agencies is, Are they performing a biblical function that builds up the body of Christ?

The fact that all believers, whenever possible, are to relate to other believers in a local congregation does not mean that the local congregation has an exclusive right over an individual's ministry. Because of this, a para-local church has two clear ministry options. First, it can legitimately become or spawn local congregations which meet the broader needs of the people. It then ceases to be a para-local church society. Some para-local church groups become de facto local churches. One Christian leader argued that "they should come out of the closet and admit that they are really churches." The other option is for para-local church groups to remain as specialists and for their members to be a part of a local church.

An individual believer can minister and express his gifts in many ways. A perfectly legitimate way is in the structure of a para-local church group. In so doing he still must bear his personal, scriptural responsibilities to his local congregation.

What about the conflict of authority? In the New Testament, we see the main application of authority in the area of personal life and discipline, not in ministry. Whatever ministry a believer performs can and should be claimed as an extension of his local fellowship. A local fellowship should provide personal and family accountability for all of its people. Yet the ministries of those same people may be diverse. Local congregations need to worry less about the ministries some of their people are involved in outside the church structure, and worry more about how to equip the larger number (perhaps the majority) of the congregation to do *some* ministry. We need to be building up the entire body of Christ, not just our own group. That applies both to local churches and para-local church groups. We spend far too much time worrying about non-existent boundaries.

There is another approach to this issue that I have purposely avoided to this point. That is the concept of local and mobile parts of the body of Christ. This concept has some real merit in demonstrating a pattern in the New Testament. However, it is not the primary validation of the legitimacy of the para-local church.

Much has been written on this two-structure concept, especially by Ralph Winter, so I will give only a brief summary. The bibliography lists a number of key references on this topic.

As we study the book of Acts (which is illustrative, not necessarily normative) we observe a mixture of local and mobile structures. At the beginning of the great missionary movements in Acts 13, we see the initiation of a series of mobile missionary teams. Edward Murphy lists them as:

> Barnabas–Saul–Mark team (13:4-13)
> Paul–Barnabas and their companions team (13:13-15:12)
> Paul–Barnabas–Judas–Silas team (15:22-34)
> Paul–Silas team (15:40f.)

Barnabas–Mark team (15:37-39)
Paul–Silas–Timothy team (16:1-9)
Paul–Silas–Timothy–Luke team (16:10f.)
Paul – Silas – Timothy – Luke – Aquila – Priscilla–
Apollos team (18:24-28)
Paul – Silas – Timothy – Luke – Erastus – Gaius–
Aristarchus team (19)
Paul –Silas–Timothy–Luke–Sopater–Aristarchus–
Secundus–Gaius–Tychicus–Trophimus team (20:4)[10]

Van Gelder observes, with reference to Winter, "that once Barnabas and Paul were sent out by the Antioch church, they were basically on their own. They were neither under the control of Antioch in decision making, nor were they dependent upon Antioch for financial support."[11] He also notes that there were "at least 30 mobile men sent out from 14 different local assemblies, other than the twelve apostles, who worked apart from, alongside of and with Paul."[12] These teams were semi-autonomous.

An interesting example is Philip. He was a deacon (Acts 6:5), not an apostle. He was sent out by an angel of the Lord to lead the Ethiopian eunuch to Christ (Acts 8:26-39). He went on "preaching the gospel in all the towns . . ." (Acts 8:40). In Acts 21:8, he is referred to as "Philip the evangelist." He was a specialized, gifted, mobile man. He was a lay missionary pursuing God's calling. He was also semi-autonomous in his pursuits.

Ephesians 4:1-16 offers verification of the mobile-local and specialized ministries. The total building up of the body of Christ (v. 12) and the working together of each individual part (v. 16) is the result of the balanced contribution of the apostles, prophets, evangelists, and pastor-teachers (v. 11).

Apostles and evangelists are generally mobile while the others are generally local. Winter and others consider the modern apostolic function to be that of a missionary or "sent one." Mobile teams planted new local assemblies and built up believers in existing congregations (*see* Acts 15:36). Although it is difficult to prove the exact categorization of the functions in Ephesians 4:11, that passage clearly demonstrates a varied and specialized contribution to the total work of God in the world.

In describing the interrelationship between the local and mobile, Winter states, "Thus, on the one hand, the structure we call the *New Testament church* is a prototype of all subsequent Christian fellowship where old and young, male and female are gathered together as normal biological families in aggregate. On the other hand, Paul's *missionary band* can be considered as a prototype of all subsequent missionary endeavors organized out of committed, experienced workers who affiliated themselves as a second decision beyond membership in the first structure."[13] Note that the intent is not to abandon the local church, but to have a dual relationship in which one functions both in a local church and in a mobile or specialist fashion. This can be as true of full-time workers as of lay participants.

There are many differences in the two structures (which we refer to as local church and para-local church rather than local and mobile). The local church is broad, concerned with the total person, ministers in a geographical locale to a wide spectrum of ages and needs, and is narrow in doctrinal interpretation. The para-local church society is usually narrow in purpose, specialized in task, narrow in the age of those involved, broad in doctrinal tolerations, crosses denominational lines (except for denominational para-local church structures), and often is geographically scattered.

One reason for our appeal to the broader concept of the body of Christ, rather than just the local-mobile concept, is that many para-local church structures are not misson sending agencies, whereas the mobile structure in Winter's work focuses mainly on missions. Ephesians 4:11-12, as well as the view of the broader body of Christ, includes all ministries outside the structure of the local congregation. Building up the body of Christ is the focus, not geography.

This analysis does not give carte blanche or complete authorization to any and every para-local church society. Each needs to be judged on the basis of its contribution to the body. Nor does it validate every local congregation since the existence of a local church in no way makes it necessary or effective. It too must be evaluated. More on that in later chapters.

Finally, we note that participation in a para-local church society causes one to function in at least two authority structures. These will occasionally be in conflict. But to have conflicting authorities—work, family, government—is not unusual. In conflict, the believer-priest is individually responsible for deciding which authority takes precedence. In the New Testament we observe local church authority applied negatively only for personal discipline, never to restrict a ministry (recall the illustration of Paul and his communication with the Jerusalem church, Acts 15 and Galatians 2:1-10). Counsel, encouragement, and prayer are valid inputs. Control is not.

SUMMARY

Both the local church and the para-local church groups comprise vital and viable parts of the body of Christ. The para-local church finds its theological legitimacy in the freedom of form given in the New Testament, in the necessary expression of each believer-priest in his ministry, and in the examples of local and mobile functions of the universal church. The local church is God's basic medium for meeting the broad needs of people of all ages and in all situations. The mobile para-local church structure is God's method for the two-fold task of missions and specialized ministries.

At times the functions will overlap, but this need not cause conflict if our goal is the upbuilding of the body, not the claiming of rights and prerogatives. All believers should be part of a local fellowship. When these believers are also involved in a para-local church ministry, there may be times of conflicting authority. But authority conflict is a frequent factor in many areas of life, and will become a problem only when one of the authorities insists that his authority has preeminence. The responsibility to choose between two loyalties lies with the individual believer-priest.

Some para-local church groups establish de facto churches on the local level. This is a legitimate outcome, but as a practice it will change the focus and effectiveness of a specialized society. A para-local church organization that wishes to keep its effectiveness should normally remain with its special calling or else it will become another denomination, as we have seen from church history.

Chapter 3, Notes

1. Although developed independently, this view is similar to that of Howard Snyder in *The Problem of Wineskins* (Downers Grove, Ill: InterVarsity Press, 1975), p. 166.

2. Ralph Winter, "The Two Structures of God's Redemptive Mission," *Missiology* 2 (January 1974): 121-39.

3. Earl D. Radmacher, *What the Church Is All About* (Chicago: Moody Press, 1978), p. 187.

4. Radmacher, *Church*, p. 189.

5. Radmacher, *Church*, p. 188.

6. Radmacher, *Church*, p. 318.

7. Francis A. Schaeffer, *The Complete Works of Francis A. Schaeffer*, vol. 4: *A Christian View of the Church* (Westchester, Ill.: Crossway Books, 1982), pp. 59-60.

8. Schaeffer, *Christian View of the Church*, p. 301, chap. 4, n. 1.

9. Schaeffer, *Christian View of the Church*, p. 54.

10. Edward F. Murphy, "The Missionary Society as an Apostolic Team," *Missiology* 4:101-18.

11. Craig Van Gelder, "Local and Mobile: A Study of Two Functions," (Jackson, Miss.: Reformed Theological Seminary, 1975), p. 24.

12. Van Gelder, "Local and Mobile," p. 25.

13. Winter, "Two Structures," pp. 122-23.

"For where you have envy and selfish ambition, there you find disorder and every evil practice. But the wisdom that comes from heaven is first of all pure; then peace loving, considerate, submissive, full of mercy and good fruits, impartial and sincere."
James 3:16-17

Chapter 4

A Perspective on Weaknesses

*A*ll human organizations have weaknesses and limitations. Both the local church and para-local church groups are human organizations. Consequently, both not only contribute to the kingdom of God, but in some ways they also hinder its work.

Because each local congregation and each para-local church organization also vary in effectiveness, generalizations become risky. But when we view the work of God in today's society, some problems clearly emerge in both structures. Weaknesses are common to both. As we review some of those weaknesses, we must not become discouraged or defensive. We need to face reality and work to make corrections whenever we can. Remember also that weaknesses are often the natural counterpoints to strengths.

WAYS PARA-LOCAL CHURCH GROUPS HINDER

LACK OF ACCOUNTABILITY

"The major criticism, and one that is easiest to make stick, is that [parachurch groups] lack accountability to anyone but themselves. Parachurch groups are religion gone free enterprise."[1]

"But sad to say, today we need not look far to find a parachurch leader who announces that he is answerable 'only to God.' "[2]

Accountability varies greatly from organization to organization. Some have active, involved boards. Others have passive, permissive boards. Larger para-local church groups tend to have checks and balances within their own staff. The smaller groups usually have greater freedom.

The introduction of the Evangelical Council for Financial Accountability (ECFA) will have a restraining and standardizing effect on member organizations, especially in financial areas. But this still does not speak to the need for accountability in effectiveness of ministry. Who determines whether or not a group is effective?

Every para-local church organization should know why it exists and have some means of measuring its effectiveness. Being a godly person or having noble purposes is not sufficient to warrant support. What is the expected result? How much does it cost? Is it being done well?

"A few groups joined the Council (ECFA) with little or no change . . . others have altered their behavior patterns significantly . . . still others have steadfastly refused disclosure. If ECFA continues to gain strength, this refusal should prove costly. It is only fair to assume that the groups refusing to disclose have more to hide than those who oblige. There is no way to restrain the less productive ministries other than through the influence of a more informed donor."[3]

The Evangelical Council for Financial Accountability will probably restrain the proliferation of para-local church groups.

NONSUPPORT OF THE LOCAL CHURCH

A perennial problem of para-local church societies has been their relationship with and support of the local church. One of the ways this becomes apparent is in the preparation and transfer of their converts and followers to the local church (provided they have transferable "fruit" rather than a service or product). Radmacher states the issue well:

In recent years there has been a tendency among some Christian enterprises, which received their material and resources from the local church, to fail to maintain a reciprocal relationship with the local church. Failing to recognize the centrality of the local church in carrying out God's program, some have failed to inculcate a healthy respect for the local church in the minds of their converts. . . . Fortunately, among some of these "arms of the church" there has been a wholesome emphasis on the centrality of the local church.[4]

Para-local church groups differ so widely generalizations cannot be totally accurate. Historical evidence validates the concern that a conscious effort needs to be made to help converts and followers make the transition to a local congregation in a healthy, productive manner. If this is not done, the earlier work of the para-local church group is greatly diminished. Also, if these people do not make the transition, the para-local church then becomes their local church and the focus of the para-local church group will be changed. A lack of concern for this issue will widen the gap between local churches and para-local church groups.

DUPLICATION AND LACK OF COORDINATION

Most para-local church groups operate in complete independence and isolation from each other. Consequently many groups duplicate and overlap each other in their specialties. This happens even in the same geographical areas. Each group thinks that its approach is unique or more effective than others—and especially more effective than the local church.

In some cases, true competition between groups develops as one group invades another's territory. Youngren observes some of the effects of this proliferation:

We are seeking to understand why so many would-be leaders act autonomously rather than under formal church authority. We are not focusing here on the 1,000 or so parachurch groups who are daily ministering effectively in Christ's name. Rather, we are dealing with the other 9,000 groups. They are the fruit of this proliferation. Their effect is like that of algae in the fish pond: when they have multiplied enough, everything around them will be killed off.[5]

Obviously, there must be a point of saturation in this proliferation process. Just like there is a limit to the number of service stations a community can support or the number of local churches that can survive, so there will be a limit to the number of para-local church groups. Some will die. Perhaps better coordination and cooperation would prevent at least some of the duplication of effort and expenditure of funds.

FOCUS ON A PERSON

Most para-local church organizations begin, and often continue, centered around a person. This person usually has a strong personality with drive and leadership. Particularly with small organizations, the total organization may be one man or woman, so the focus is on supporting that person and his or her vision. If the organization grows, it generally continues to center around the personality of its founder-leader. We can point to many organizations where the original leader still wields an authoritative influence.

If the focus is on the person rather than on Christ, the true focus of the ministry will disappear and a personality cult will result. A personality-centered organization will greatly hinder the work of Christ in the world. Some ministries can even emerge as an ego satisfaction for one who cannot function under the leadership of others and needs "his own work" to feel fulfilled. Such a motive will not have God's blessing.

LACK OF BALANCE

One pastor has said, "The New Testament concept of the church is not invisible, but it's basically local, specific and identifiable. The parachurch agencies do not provide the needed balance and they become an excuse for noninvolvement with a local body of believers."[6]

As specialists, most para-local church societies only focus on part of a believer's total need—counseling, discipleship, evangelism training, Bible study, seminary training, and others. Rarely does one para-local church group meet the total needs of a person. These groups may magnify their specialty beyond its normal proportion in the body. Para-local church staff and leaders need to keep their ministry in perspective with the whole body of Christ, and need to teach their members to balance the specialized training they receive with other important aspects of growth and ministry. However, when an organization attempts to be balanced and meet the entire set of needs of an individual, they become a de facto local church. They must walk a tightrope between the extremes.

FEW DEATHS

Constant births of new para-local church organizations along with few deaths is one factor producing the great explosion of organizations. "In the not-for-profit world of such agencies, almost no organization ever goes out of existence. . . . No forces seem to operate to eliminate the unproductive and ineffective group, or the group that has exhausted its usefulness or fully accomplished its purpose. This is in sharp contrast to the for-profit world in which the weak yield what they have to the strong and then succumb, purging the system as they themselves are purged."[7]

Though this may be an overstatement, the fact still persists that groups do not die easily even if they are not now, or ever were, effective. If donors keep giving, the group keeps going. Para-local church organizations need to periodically review their reasons for being. Some groups need to join forces with others. Some need to close down. One person's vision is not sufficient reason to keep functioning; there also needs to be the obvious hand of God upon the work.

WAYS LOCAL CHURCHES HINDER

Not every local church is effective. Just as some para-local church groups hinder the work of God, so some local churches hinder it also. Both structures have their critics—and their obvious weaknesses. The renewal and church growth movements of today point to some of the real needs of the local church.

DUPLICATION, PARTY SPIRIT, AND LACK OF UNITY

Howard Snyder begins his book, *The Problem of Wineskins,* with the startling statement, "It is hard to escape the conclusion that today one of the greatest roadblocks to the gospel of Jesus Christ is the institutional church."[8]

As the world looks at the evangelical church they see a feisty, fighting, and divided establishment. Church denominations often plan their strategies for new churches without regard for other groups ministering in the area. They are considered competition, not co-workers. The party spirit of being the "true New Testament church" permeates the interchurch scene to such a degree that any cooperation that does occur is superficial and ineffective. The independence and autonomy of a local congregation, carried to the extreme, produces a negative witness to the community.

There is almost total duplication in many geographical areas. To non-Christians and new believers, the picture is one of confusion and arguments over minor issues. Obviously, they are not minor to those holding rigidly to various distinctives, but to the outside world they appear inconsequential. Many churches have destroyed their testimony in their community by infighting and splits. What little interest the world has in spiritual matters is hindered by this confusion, argument, and division.

The question, "Which church is the church of your city?" still needs to be addressed.

FOCUS ON BUILDINGS

Almost everyone agrees that the local church is not a building. But almost every local church spends a vast amount of time, energy, and money on buildings. Even when we know better, we use the words "church" and "going to church," with reference to a building. Brick and mortar become a holy place. The emphasis on a sanctuary, "coming into the presence of God," or even quietness in the meeting room all focus on the building as a sacred place rather than a functional tool for the ministry of the local church.

Snyder sharply points out our improper focus and its basis.

> The three central elements in the Mosaic Covenant were sacrifice, priesthood and tabernacle . . . all instituted through Moses in the Old Testament. Theologically, all passed away with the coming of Christ and the birth of the church. . . .
>
> And so the church was born without priesthood, sacrifice or tabernacle because the church and Christ together were all three. . . .
>
> The great temptation of the organized church has been to reinstate these three elements among God's people: to turn community into an insitution. Historically, the church has at times succumbed. Returning to the spirit of the Old Testament, she has set up a professional priesthood, turned the Eucharist into a new sacrifical system and built great cathedrals.[9]

The tabernacle and temple are no more. Jesus told the Samaritan woman that the temple at Jerusalem would be replaced and worship would be "in spirit and truth" (John 4:7-24). Yet we still try to designate a *place* of worship. Such an overemphasis hinders the true form of the church in the world.

Perhaps one of the greatest sins of churches today is the vast amount of money spent on buildings as compared to the amount spent on missions. Is it really necessary and right to spend on a building as much as or more than the church gives to missions in a ten year period?

CLERGY / LAITY DIVISIONS

The tendency to return to the priesthood is seen throughout history. Even in evangelical circles we see an emphasis on a professional clergy—a priest-substitute—and the consequent separation of clergy and laity. The sharp distinction hinders the true understanding of the body of Christ. To have full-time pastors certainly is not wrong. But the way we in this age have highlighted the position is a hindrance.

LACK OF FLEXIBILITY

The church is one of the slowest institutions in society to change. It is immovable (although not by the forces of Satan) simply because it becomes petrified in its structure. Attempting to bring about significant, not to mention radical, change in most local churches is a suicidal mission. It is usually easier to start a new church. And that is often what happens. To prevent this proliferation of new churches, we need the flexibility "to work out a structure which fits our new and changing world—one which blends into a culture built on the car and the jet, on the TV and the moving van; not one built on the old gray mare."[10]

"And there must be a freedom under the leadership of the Holy Spirit to change what needs to be changed, to meet the changing needs in that place and in the moment of that situation. Otherwise, I do not believe there is a place for the church as a living church. We will be ossified, and we will shut Christ out of the church."[11] The inflexibility of the local church greatly hinders the work and witness of God and its effectiveness in the lives of believers—especially new believers.

LACK OF RELEVANCE AND IMPACT IN A PAGAN CULTURE

The American culture is changing at an increasingly fast rate. And the church is becoming less and less of a dynamic force in that culture. Even in a country where over one-third claim to be born again, the relevance gap is widening. Humanism and secularism have so engulfed the younger generation that the "bring them to the church" concept no longer has any possibility of working.

The nonbeliever's view of the local church and its people holds no attraction for him. He views them as totally unrelated to the realities of his life and experience. The church scattered into the marketplace, understanding the issues and moving more cautiously in their attempts to draw the unchurched into the institution, forms the only hope. The continuing insistence that new converts must be rapidly related to the institutional church will increasingly hinder its effectiveness in the world.

FOCUS ON A PERSON

Some of the most successful churches today have been founded and built by one man. Without that man, the congregation would disperse. As helpful as great teachers are, they do not make the church effective. The emphasis on the superstar pastor makes the church an audience, not a body.[12] It is a deceptive form of a functioning local church. Not that a large church with a highly gifted pastor cannot be a functioning local body, but that pastor's importance tends to so overshadow the system that other areas may not receive the proper attention and priority. Even a small church can focus on a person, rather than on the function of the body. Size is not the issue. The work of God is hindered where Christians are drawn to a local church by the wrong magnet—a personality rather than the living community of believers.

LACK OF ACCOUNTABILITY

There is no Evangelical Council for Financial Accountability for the local church. Its accountability is totally inward to its own people who may have little knowledge of how to manage a local church. (By contrast, outsiders must form the majority on the boards of ECFA members.) Who really evaluates a local church's effectiveness? The only time real votes are cast is when people leave or a pastor is fired. Seldom does an outside auditor examine a local church's books.

From Scripture we know that accountability is to be placed in a group of elders. But what about the many local churches where the elders do not meet the scriptural qualifications or where they simply do not function in an accountable fashion, either spiritually or financially? Ted Engstrom points out that local churches devote 80 percent of their income to overhead expenditures, and less than 20 percent to overseas missions or local community outreach programs. Any other group with those figures would be subject to severe criticism. Add a building program to the picture and inward expenditures increase even more.[13]

FEW DEATHS

Finally, as in the case of para-local church groups, we rarely see a local church die. It may be totally ineffective or theologically invalid, but it still goes on, a shell with no life. Does the existence of a local church for a hundred years give it the right to continue functioning even when it is ineffective? Must we always attempt to give artificial respiration to a congregation that is clinically dead? Its greatest contribution may be to close down, sell the property, and give the proceeds to foreign missions.

SUMMARY

Both local churches and para-local church groups have needs and problems. Neither gets a clean bill of health. While individual churches or groups may do a superb job of ministry, that is not the case with all. We must recognize the shortcomings of both.

But our tendency is to view our own local church or para-local church group through rose-colored glasses. We fail to see our own needs, or the broader needs of either the local church or para-local church structure. Somehow we think if we are doing "God's work in God's way," human frailties will not detour God's purpose. Experience and history tell us a different story.

Rather than being discouraged or defensive, let us do what we can to make corrections and get on with the work of God where we are. We cannot fight the battles and problems of any other church or group but our own.

Chapter 4, Notes

1. Stephen Board, "The Great Evangelical Power Shift," *Eternity*, June 1979, p. 17.

2. J. Alan Youngren, "Parachurch Proliferation: The Frontier Spirit Caught in Traffic," *Christianity Today*, Nov. 6, 1981, p. 39.

3. Youngren, "Parachurch Proliferation," p. 41.

4. Earl D. Radmacher, *What the Church Is All About* (Chicago: Moody Press, 1978), p. 364.

5. Youngren, "Parachurch Proliferation," p. 39.

6. Board, "Power Shift," p. 17.

7. Youngren, "Parachurch Proliferation," p. 39.

8. Howard A. Snyder, *The Problem of Wineskins* (Downers Grove, Ill.: Inter-Varsity Press, 1975), p. 21.

9. Snyder, *Wineskins*, pp. 57-58.

10. Lawrence O. Richards, *A New Face for the Church* (Grand Rapids: Zondervan Publishing House, 1970), p. 144.

11. Francis A. Schaeffer, *The Complete Works of Francis A. Schaeffer*, vol. 4: *A Christian View of the Church* (Westchester, Ill.: Crossway Books, 1982), p. 68.

12. Snyder, *Wineskins*, p. 83.

13. Ted W. Engstrom, "Is Overhead a Waste of Money?", *Eternity*, April 1976, pp. 24-25.

"There is one body and one Spirit—just as you were called to one hope when you were called—one Lord, one faith, one baptism; one God and Father of all, who is over all and through all and in all."
Ephesians 4:4-6

Chapter 5

Assessing Where We Are

*I*n chapter 1, I proposed four issues as the main areas of conflict and concern. Each of them reflects actual experience over the years, and each needs to be understood and resolved.

PEOPLE (LEADERSHIP)

People, especially gifted leaders, are always in short supply. There will always be some competition for their talents. Some people have a large capacity and are able to participate in both a local church and a para-local church, making a good contribution in each. But others are limited in their capacities and must emphasize one over the other.

We must be careful to allow each person the God-given freedom to use his gifts to the greatest extent, and to make his special contribution to the body of Christ. If our major concern is that people are serving God and are spiritually productive, we will not be so concerned about whether or not they are operating in our particular ministry context. This becomes especially difficult for the local church since people often remain involved there while giving their primary service to a para-local church group.

Patience needs to be exercised. Rarely will a person remain deeply involved with a para-local church group over several years. In all likelihood, they will be available to the church later and will make an even more significant contribution after their para-local church training. But they will not do that in a church that communicated its disapproval while they were ministering elsewhere. They need encouragement from the local church, and must feel a part of its outreach.

Concern has been expressed that people may be staying away from local churches in favor of involvement with para-local church groups. Some pastors become quite upset if people miss a Sunday service to be in a para-local church conference or training session. In reality, when else could such conferences be held? A less possessive attitude would greatly free people to get such help, and ultimately the local church would benefit from their training.

I agree with the analysis that "there is no good evidence that people are staying away from churches in droves while they resort to parachurch alternatives. More likely, a few key people are unavailable for a few key jobs in the local church because of their outside activities. Understandably, this annoys the pastor."[1]

I suggest that local churches survey their members to determine where they became believers and where they received help in personal growth. Ask specifics about their past involvements in para-local church societies. I think the results will show that many received Christ in a para-local church group, and that one-third to one-half have been influenced positively. In churches where such involvement is discouraged, the percentage will likely be less. Churches that encourage and approve of para-local church groups will benefit in receiving a much greater portion of the members of those groups.

THEOLOGY (LEGITIMACY)

Since I devoted an entire chapter to this topic, I will say little more here. Chapter 3 attempts to demonstrate that both local church structures and para-local church structures are valid parts of the body of Christ that have experienced God's blessing throughout history.

FINANCES (MONEY)

Money, especially lack of it, sends emotional tremors through any local church. A number of pastors believe that para-local church groups drain a significant amount of money from the local church. Attempting to gather accurate figures on the amount of money flowing to both structures is like counting all the sparrows in the United States—virtually impossible! Only data from major denominations are available. This leaves thousands of independent churches unaccounted for. The data for the para-local church groups are equally difficult to find. Members of the Evangelical Council for Financial Accountability form only a part of the total number. Thousands of small organizations (unknown to most people) cannot be accounted for.

However, some analysis can be done from sample organizations and churches, and from published financial data. That analysis yields the following:

1. Of the total contributions to Protestant causes, 9.7 percent is given directly to para-local church organizations and not channelled through the local church.
2. Of the total contributions to local churches, 2.2 percent goes to Protestant para-local church organizations.

Since there is some uncertainty in the figures, we will round them to 10 and 2 percent. This gives us a total of 12 percent of all Protestant giving going to Protestant para-local church agencies. Due to the "softness" of the available data, I estimate the percentages to lie between a minimum of 10 percent and a maximum of 13 percent.[2]

This is less than many people would have predicted. At the same time, it is a large amount of money. To balance this, we must consider the increased giving to churches that comes from members and former members of para-local church groups. Most of these people have been taught to give early in their Christian experience, and often transfer their giving to the local church. Though impossible to measure, I suspect it is significant. It would be interesting to compare their giving to the local church with that of the rest of the congregation.

Some interesting financial facts came out of my survey of pastors. Fifty percent believed in "storehouse tithing." Eighty percent felt that the para-local church movement was *not* a major drain on their churches' finances. Of those surveyed, 91 percent had people in the congregation who had been significantly influenced by para-local church groups.

I conclude that the financial issue is not nearly as significant as many people have surmised. Even though the amount going to para-local church groups is somewhere between 10 and 13 percent of total giving, that probably is canceled out by the gain in income to the local church due to the influx of para-local church people.

AUTHORITY (LOYALTIES)

A believer is frequently faced with conflicting authorities. But authority conflicts only become an issue in the church when someone decides to minister outside the local church structure. Authority is rarely exerted in other areas of members' lives. The large number of people who do little or no ministry—in or out of the local church—is hardly affected at all. If authority is exercised over people's ministry, it should be to get them *to begin* ministry, not to restrict those who are already doing it.

Additionally, the New Testament does not record restrictive authority being exercised in any area but church discipline.

The concept that all ministry, whether of individuals or groups, should be under the authority of a local church or denomination simply does not have scriptural support. Certainly elders hold some spiritual authority, but primarily over areas of personal life. Local church authority extends to ministry issues only when the individual has voluntarily placed himself under that authority. In fact, no authority can really be exercised without the consent of the individual. Even so, para-local church groups need to be more sensitive to the existing loyalties of people in the local church. And local church leaders need to accept the fact that people in their congregations will have outside loyalties as well. No pastor or para-local church leader should expect blind loyalty or obedience, particularly if his church or group is not meeting people's needs. No local church can expect loyalty just because it is a church. Hebrews 13:17 instructs us to obey our leaders, and submit to their authority. This assumes that they truly do "keep watch over [us]." And Hebrews 13:7 teaches that we follow leaders as we observe their conduct or way of life. Blind obedience is never the biblical expectation.

CONTRIBUTIONS OF PARA-LOCAL CHURCH GROUPS

Almost without exception, pastors recognize that God is using the para-local church movement.

In my own survey of pastors, 53 percent indicated their belief that para-local church organizations are making a significant contribution to the kingdom of God today. Of the remaining 47 percent, all acknowledged that some para-local church groups are contributing significantly.

In his fine work, *The Church Unleashed*, Pastor Frank Tillapaugh comments,

> Parachurch ministries have been around for a long time; some would argue that they go back to the New Testament. But most of the best known and most active organizations have come into existence since the late 1930s. Inter-Varsity is the oldest of a long and impressive list including the Navigators, Campus Crusade for Christ, Youth for Christ, Young Life, International Students, Inc., Child Evangelism, Teen Challenge, Jews for Jesus, Fellowship of Christian Athletes, plus dozens of others. Why have so many of these types of organizations come into existence in the past forty years? . . . I believe the primary positive reason is that God has raised them up."[3]

Tillapaugh shows how the local church has become a "Fortress Church," withdrawn behind the walls of its buildings while para-local church groups have penetrated society out in the battlefield. He then pleads for the local church to learn from these societies and apply the appropriate principles to their own structure. But what can be learned? Where have para-local church organizations led the way and made significant contributions?

MISSIONS

In the last two centuries, the mission thrust has largely been initiated and developed by independent mission agencies. Denominational agencies (also para-local church by my definition) have developed and been fruitful as well, but the initiative came from individuals who saw a need, tried to convince the institutional church to help meet the need, and finally ventured out on their own.

The cutting edge of missions still rests with the independent societies, although conservative denominational groups are intensely involved too. The church growth movement has been a key factor, along with several schools of world missions that have injected new life into Bible schools and seminaries.

MOBILIZATION OF THE LAITY

The core of the para-local church movement is lay people. The genius of the movement has been its willingness and ability to use, train, and involve lay men and women. The seeming inability of the local church to give status and motivation to the laity has blocked the arteries of the institutional church, despite the valiant efforts of men like Gene Getz and Ray Stedman.

Para-local church groups lead people to Christ, feed hungry and willing lay people, give them a tool, and send them to the harvest field. One person doing the work is better than hundreds wanting to be used but finding no available training or ministry vehicle.

PLACE FOR WOMEN

Through the years, mission agencies and other para-local church organizations have equipped and sent women—married and single—to the harvest fields of the world. Even today a large percentage of the missionary force is single women. Most para-local church groups have women on their full-time staffs because they are effective—God is obviously using them.

This recognition of the contribution of women preceded by years any women's liberation movement. Women's ministry does not have anything to do with rights or liberation, but with fulfilling the great commission and putting workers into the harvest fields.

EVANGELISM

Evangelism in our increasingly pagan culture requires penetration, not bombardment from a fortress. Para-local church organizations have become experts in penetration. They evangelize in the midst of the market place, and develop effective methods of lay witness. They do evangelism *and* train people how to do it. They penetrate specialized cultural and ethnic groups, such as youth, students, people in nonevangelical churches, and military personnel.

In addition, large scale or mass evangelism has had a great impact on our country. In spite of criticisms leveled at mass evangelism, the results of it are clearly evident. People do receive Christ. The gospel is presented to many who would never enter the door of the institutional church. In addition to the well-known ministry of Billy Graham, there are many others who have effective crusades on a smaller scale or within groups of churches. From the time of Moody to today, mass evangelism has been a significant para-local church function.

INSTRUCTION AND TRAINING IN MINISTRY SKILLS

Specialist para-local church groups concentrate on teaching people how to be effective ministers as believer-priests. For example, Tillapaugh observes, "if you say to anyone trained by the Navigators, 'There's an apartment complex; let's have a ministry there,' he knows what you mean and he knows what to do. . . . On the other hand, if you were to say to the average Baptist or Presbyterian, 'There's an apartment complex; let's have a ministry there,' he would have no idea what you meant. Because he thinks of ministry as some form of church work. And church work happens inside a church building."[4]

In today's world, the effective, growing church will be one that mobilizes and trains laymen, and encourages them to work outside, as well as inside, the church structure. This is equipping believers for the work of the ministry. Para-local church groups have long concentrated on providing instruction and training for these ministry skills.

DISCIPLESHIP AND PERSONAL GROWTH

Much of the renewed emphasis on discipleship stems from a number of the discipleship-focused para-local church societies. For many years these groups have emphasized personal growth through person-to-person and group discipleship, and personal Bible study. The strong emphasis on obeying the Word of God, on taking responsibility for one's life, on being renewed in one's spiritual life, and on living a holy, fruitful life is making its impact on the body of Christ.

Books, Bible study materials, seminars, and many other methods come through para-local church channels. Wise church leaders acquire these helps and use them in their congregations. Such emphasis relates back to the early student movements, the Keswick influence, and the personal discipleship groups of the fifties and sixties.

SMALL GROUP CONCEPT

Para-local church societies generally have few large buildings or facilities in relation to their number of staff. Their stock in trade is the small group. From prayer meetings and Bible studies to training seminars, the believer is built up in the informal, small group atmosphere. Forward thinking local church innovators have long recognized the importance of small fellowship groups, but have found it difficult to implement the small group concept in a congregation of mixed needs and backgrounds.

Para-local church groups are generally more homogeneous in composition, background, age, and needs, so small groups develop more easily. The warmth of personal relationships that develop in these small groups fosters biblical fellowship and growth in a way that a large church meeting can never achieve. Also, the communication of a vision for ministry is facilitated by the encouragement and support of the small group. Churches need to adapt and adopt these methods. Certainly para-local church groups have not been the sole proponents of these methods. They have functioned in the church for centuries. But para-local church groups have capitalized on their use in an unprecedented way.

EDUCATION

Many of our finest educational institutions at the elementary, high school, college, and graduate levels are para-local church movements. The Christian school movement of the last fifteen years could never have happened without visionary people outside the institutional church taking the risks of countering some of the problems in the public school system. Many of these schools were formed by laymen in local churches, but not under the direct authority of one church. Other educational endeavors have denominational ties, but they are not a local church nor are they local church controlled.

Add to this the host of fine independent seminaries and Bible schools, and one sees the great impact of the movement. Additionally, other para-local church groups contribute significant numbers to the student bodies of these schools. Estimates of the proportion of evangelical seminary students whose roots go back to para-local church groups range from 25 to 50 percent.[5] Many of these students later go into the ministry of the local church.

INNOVATION

The para-local church is an ideal proving ground for experimentation and the testing of new ideas. Institutional churches change slowly and are rarely innovative. Rather, others promote new ideas that, once tested, are then adapted to the local church. That cooperation proves to be a good partnership and provides a significant contribution to the body of Christ.

The Future of the Para-Local Church

Para-local church organizations are here to stay. They will be a growing, significant influence in the next half century. Their ultimate permanence is known only to God. From the historical perspective of the last three hundred years, their development has been steady, with explosive growth in the last thirty years.

Such rapid proliferation may not continue, but para-local church structures are here to stay for the foreseeable future. Historically, when new denominational movements emerged, people predicted they would disappear in due time or would fulfill their goal and return to the current establishment. But they did not. They are still with us today as denominations.

The form and structure of para-local church organizations may change, just as the form and structure of local churches change. Some para-local church groups will develop into new denominations or spawn local congregations. Others will continue to grow in their specialist role, varying in method rather than vision or goal. Others will die a natural death. But most para-local church groups will continue to grow and be innovators in the body of Christ.

Cooperation and interrelationships will grow between para-local church groups and those local churches that sanction and support their existence. Otherwise, economic demands will force para-local church groups to become even more independent of local congregations.

Mission sending will continue to be dominated by independent para-local church structures, and denominational mission agencies will continue to diminish. In 1969, church related mission societies led independent societies by a 53 percent to 47 percent margin. In 1972 the *independent* mission societies led by a 53 to 47 percent margin. That gap continued to grow to 59 percent to 41 percent by 1975.[6] More recent data reflects the same trends. Mission initiatives today come principally from independent societies. The freedom in independent societies to innovate and adjust gives them an advantage.

The local church will also continue to grow and change as it attempts to meet the needs of our culture. The larger churches will adopt some of the specialties practiced by para-local church groups, and, in essence, develop para-local church groups in miniature within their own structures. Local churches that remain inflexible and unwilling to adapt structure and methods will experience a decreasing effectiveness, and will be replaced by other local congregations in their geographical areas.

Summary

Para-local church structures have made a significant contribution to the body of Christ in spite of the struggles and conflicts over their acceptance. They are not just a stepchild of the local church, but contributing partners to the work of the kingdom of God.

But the future must hold more acceptance, approval, and cooperation between para-local church organizations and the local church. The movement is so large that if this is not done, the para-local church will simply spawn its own congregations, resulting in more divisions, more denominations, more associations. The loser in that process will be the entire body of Christ. For the sake of the kingdom, the local church must not be further divided, and the para-local church must not be hindered in its specialist mission and mode.

Chapter 5, Notes

1. Stephen Board, "The Great Evangelical Power Shift," *Eternity*, June 1979, p. 20.

2. These calculations were made by Donald McGilchrist using a typical para-local church agency and a typical proagency local church (which gave 6 percent to para-local church agencies). The atypical aspects were factored out and combined with data from: *The Yearbook of American and Canadian Churches*, edited by Constance H. Jaquet, Jr. (Nashville: Abingdon Press, 1982), pp. 248-49; and *The Mission Handbook: North American Protestant Ministries Overseas*, 12th ed., edited by Samuel Wilson (Monrovia, Calif.: MARC, 1979), pp. 56-68. This does not include giving to denominational missions or organizations.

3. Frank R. Tillapaugh, *The Church Unleashed* (Ventura, Calif.; Regal Books, 1982), pp. 14-15.

4. Tillapaugh, *Church Unleashed*, p. 18.

5. This influence is reflected in a survey of seminary administrators reported in "Parachurch Fallout: Seminary Students," *Christianity Today*, Nov. 6, 1981, pp. 36-37.

6. Ralph D. Winter, "Protestant Mission Societies: The American Experience," *Missiology* 7 (April 1979): 153.

PART
2

RECOMMENDATIONS FOR RESOLVING THE PROBLEMS AND ISSUES

*"Make my joy complete by being like-minded,
having the same love, being one in spirit and purpose."*
Philippians 2:2

Chapter 6

A Proposed Solution

*F*rom all of this analysis and discussion, we need to finally come to some solutions and recommendations. All the talk or analysis in the world will not answer everyone's questions, or satisfy everyone's need for proof. The discussion and debate will probably never come to an end. But we must make significant strides toward a solution before proliferation makes the gap even wider.

I sense in both the local church and the para-local church an increased desire for mutual acceptance and understanding. As pastor Gordon MacDonald has put it, "There is so much to be excited about the parachurch turning toward the church and becoming its partner rather than its competitor."[1]

At the same time there is clearly not an anti-local church stance on the part of key para-local church leaders. In my survey of these leaders, there was a strong positive attitude toward the local church, and virtually no criticism.

Good attitudes need to be transformed into positive actions. In this chapter, I will summarize what I believe to be the key elements of a solution. These will then be expanded in the next three chapters as they apply to local congregations, para-local church groups, and participants in para-local church groups.

Key Elements

Affirm the theological legitimacy of para-local church societies. As long as shadows of doubt concerning legitimacy hang over the heads of para-local church leaders, little progress will be made toward cooperation. We are all a part of the body of Christ, and function as believer-priests in the place of God's choosing.

In chapter 3, we concluded that great freedom of structure and expression is allowed by the New Testament. As examples, we see the mobile and local expressions of the church operating in harmony and cooperation in the New Testament. The para-local church is not just a temporary gapfiller due to the failure of local churches. It is part of God's plan in this age. We need to affirm the legitimacy of both structures and get on with the task of fulfilling the Great Commission. We must learn from both the freedom of form in the New Testament and the testimony of church history that God is not restricted to our human concepts of structure. When the institutional forms present roadblocks, God discards them and raises up others in their place.

Count the para-local church as part of the legitimate ministry of the local church. Most para-local church staff and constituency are part of a local congregation. Draw them in and encourage them in their ministry, rather than make them feel they must be involved in the direct program of the church. Rejoice with them as the extension of the local body through their ministry. Give them the privileges of personal accountability and fellowship in the congregation. Both the church and the para-local church will benefit greatly.

In his excellent book, *A Theology of Personal Ministry,* Larry Richards recalls an incident from his past that broadened his perspective on the ministry of the body.

> At one time I served as the minister of education of a large Illinois church. There were vacancies on various agency staffs, so I phoned all the members of the congregation to find out if they were willing to serve. What amazed me then was the discovery that many of the

members of our congregation had personal ministries to which God had called them that were *not* associated with the programs of our church! . . .

I expressed my appreciation for the ministry they had and released them from any sense of obligation to work in our church programs. Also I began a "God at Work" column in the church newsletter, designed to let the congregation know of some of the personal ministries to which their fellow believers were called.[2]

What a beautiful attitude! And what a freeing action on behalf of the local church. Several of his congregation were involved in a para-local church ministry. Others were doing hospital calling or other individual outreaches on their own. The true ministry of the local church cannot be charted, counted, and controlled. When para-local church people sense this cooperative spirit, they will draw even closer to the local congregation. The reverse is also true. With disapproval comes separation.

Encourage significant financial involvement in para-local church ministries. All missionaries and para-local church staff feel a deeper sense of responsibility to local churches that are involved with them financially. Local churches as well would like to see greater accountability on the part of staff of para-local church organizations. One key way of fostering that sense of responsibility and accountability is for local churches to support para-local church ministries. No para-local church organization could survive on the giving they receive from churches alone. Churches supply less than 10 percent of the income for most organizations.

Local churches that support para-local church staff will certainly have an influence in their ministry. However, such support cannot be contingent on that person's personal involvement in the supporting church since the staff person can only be part of one church at a time. He or she must be treated as a missionary serving elsewhere.

Obviously local churches cannot support every person who comes and asks for financial help. I suggest setting guidelines for screening such requests. The guidelines could include such things as geography, doctrinal compatibility, effectiveness, and area of specialty. I suggest for all missionary support that churches give more money to fewer people. A ten dollar monthly gift from a church is really a very minor involvement. I suggest that churches seriously consider one hundred dollars per month as a minimum, and that some missionaries receive 50 percent of their support from one local church.

Para-local church organizations should clearly define their purposes and goals, and be willing to be evaluated. Organizations become ineffective as they compromise their vision. Para-local church societies need to know why they exist, and be able to clearly communicate their goals. They also need to demonstrate their effectiveness in some measurable way. Issues like administration, overhead, evangelistic results, utilization of staff time, staff accountability, and general financial responsibility all represent possible areas for evaluation.

Local churches should not be afraid to ask hard questions. The lack of field staff supervision by many organizations—particularly in one- or two-person para-local church groups—needs to be questioned. Those who give do need to be assured that their money is being used wisely. Finances are one of the main restraints God uses to get the attention of both local church and para-local church organizations. This does not imply that a local church should be able to control a para-local church group, but they should influence them to good stewardship and to effectiveness within their stated goals.

Para-local church staff should relate to a local congregation. All believers need to relate to a local body of believers. Para-local church staff are not an exception. They need the personal accountability and encouragement that a local church provides. One of the greatest hindrances to harmonious relations with local churches is para-local church staff who make only a token commitment to their local church.

We expect people from all walks of life to work forty to fifty hours a week, and then give time to the ministry of the local church. Para-local church staff surely can give forty to fifty hours to their own work, and still give time to the local congregation. However, such staff should not generally be the foundational leaders in a local congregation, but should help raise up local leadership in the church.

Para-local church leaders should give sound teaching on responsibility to the local congregation. Just as silent disapproval from the local church speaks volumes, so the silence of para-local church leaders communicates disapproval to their constituency. It is a two-way street. Para-local church members will seldom find their total needs met over extended periods by these organizations. As specialists, para-local church groups will meet only part of the needs. Definite efforts must be made to teach and encourage new believers to relate to a local congregation. Local church leaders need to be patient since developing this relationship is not a sudden process for those coming out of a secular context. It may take a year or more to guide people into a church relationship if they come from nonevangelical backgrounds, or if a church setting is totally foreign to them.

Nonchurch people feel very uncomfortable in the normal worship service of a church. They become confused, wondering what the purpose is for all the ritual. They experience a frustration similar to one who sees a soccer game for the first time, and tries to follow the play and understand the rules. We need to bridge new believers into the fellowship, not drag them in and hope they will survive.

Attending a Sunday worship service regularly does not insure growth. It makes some members of a local church feel better, but it may not help the new believer significantly. This will become increasingly true in our growing secular society.

Emphasize the ministry of the laity. The believer-priest is God's front-line soldier. The local church must learn how to equip and mobilize its lay people for the task of the ministry. Then when God calls them into a full-time ministry, the church should consider adding them to its staff, or encouraging them to affiliate with a para-local church group. This would provide a viable alternative to the current one-way start to the ministry through a seminary education.

How can the church afford additional staff? Why not allow them to be supported through the church on a "faith" basis. That seems better than proliferating another independent organization. What if they wish to minister beyond a single local church? Free them to do so. Why must everything only contribute to a visible result in our own local church? For those who go to para-local church groups, commission them and support them. In today's church world (with a few notable exceptions), the only ministry choices for lay men and women without seminary or Bible school training are para-local church groups.

Utilize the skills and specialties of para-local church groups to benefit the local church. Take advantage of the special contributions of para-local church groups and staff by calling on them to help the local church train its people. Most para-local church groups want to see the local church doing more, and will gladly help train people to serve in the local church.

Larger churches can stimulate specialty ministries within their own structures. Local churches can bring much of this training into their own congregations, or gain access to it by sending key people to para-local church seminars and conferences.

GUIDELINES FOR CONFLICT RESOLUTION

My goal in this book is to stimulate the process of closing the gap in one area of conflict and concern: the local church and the para-local church. But books do not resolve conflicts—people do. I believe the people involved in this issue are both godly and deeply concerned about doing what is spiritually right. I trust that the analysis and guidelines developed here will be a catalyst to greater acceptance and understanding.

In the best of situations there will be conflict. But conflict is not all bad, if it is biblically handled and resolved. When issues come up between the local church and a para-local church structure, the principals involved are usually an individual in the local church, the pastor or pastoral staff, and a staff representative of the para-local church group. Try the following process to help address and resolve the conflict.

First, address the problem as early as possible so that it will not fester and grow beyond the original issue.

Second, get the facts. Many problems are due to incorrect information passed from one person to another. Talk to the people involved—the individual, the pastor, the para-local church staff, or whoever has the facts.

Third, discuss the issue just with the individual involved since he is primarily responsible for his actions and choices.

Fourth, if the problem or conflict is not satisfactorily resolved with the individual, call the para-local church staff person (or the pastor if the issue is being pursued by the para-local church staff) and arrange a private conversation to discuss the matter.

Finally, if necessary, meet together with all the individuals involved. Make some agreements to resolve the problem or come to a mutual understanding of the issues.

Most conflicts will be resolved in this process.

At times a pastor may feel that a para-local church staff person is not responding properly or is damaging the entire para-local church group by his actions. In that case, write a letter with a summary of the facts to the organizational headquarters. Most organizations are very concerned about their relationships with local churches and will usually take steps to resolve the problem. Also send a copy of the letter to the staff person involved in order to keep everything out in the open.

SUMMARY

This proposed solution is not a "live and let live" proposal. It is a "live and encourage to live" proposal. In a time of great need for reaching out to an increasingly secular society largely belligerent to institutional Christianity, we cannot afford inner conflict and competition. We need desperately to mobilize every resource in every way to reach the lost and make disciples.

Struggles over structure, authority, and organizational rights can do nothing but repulse the onlooking world and diminish the effectiveness of the body of Christ. I believe this proposed solution can be fulfilled without a wave of watered-down ecumenicity or the forsaking of doctrinal distinctives and beliefs. But to do so, both the local church and the para-local church structures must publicly make specific efforts to encourage and help one another.

Chapter 6, Notes

1. Gordon MacDonald, "Taking Potshots at the Pastor," *Christianity Today,* July 17, 1981, pp. 52-55.

2. Lawrence O. Richards and Gib Martin, *A Theology of Personal Ministry* (Grand Rapids: Zondervan Publishing House, 1981), pp. 176-77.

"Instead, speaking the truth in love, we will in all things grow up into him who is the Head, that is, Christ. From him the whole body, joined and held together by every supporting ligament, grows and builds itself up in love, as each part does its work."
Ephesians 4:15-16

Chapter 7

Handbook for the Church

*T*he morning worship service concluded with the final hymn.
Pastor Steve Carter led the congregation in the benediction
and made his way to the door to greet people. He could recognize
visitors in the small congregation. A young couple with two small
children made their way toward him.

"Hello, I'm Pastor Steve Carter. We're glad to have you
folks visiting us today."

"Hello, Pastor Carter. I'm Don Jackson and this is my wife,
Ann, and my children, Sue and Todd."

"Ann, it's nice to have you. Are you folks new to the area?"

"Yes, we moved in last week. I'm a staff representative for
Outreach Ministries."

The pastor paused for a frozen moment of time. "I see. Uh
. . . well, please come and visit us again." All the while a rush of
questions flocked through his mind. What is Outreach Ministries?
Why are they moving here? Is it evangelical? Or he may think, "Oh
no, another parachurch organization to deal with."

That pause spoke volumes to Don and Ann. They had seen
that response before. It looked like that church might not be the
place for their family to settle. In that moment, both the church and
Don Jackson missed a great opportunity.

How could this unspoken communication have been turned into a positive communication? Pastor Carter could have continued like this.

"Outreach Ministries? I don't think I'm familiar with your organization, but I'd like to know more. Could we meet and talk sometime?"

"I'd be glad to," replied Don with an inner sigh of relief. "Our phone isn't in yet, so I'll call you Tuesday."

"I'll look forward to it. By the way, is there anything I can do to help you get settled?"

"Well, we do need to locate a physician soon. Sue's been battling allergies. In fact, that's part of the reason for our move to this area."

"When you call Tuesday, I'll give you the names of a couple of good doctors in the area. I'm sure they'll be able to help you."

Just a little acceptance goes a long way. And a little rejection lasts a long time.

Para-local church staff are often strongly motivated to relate to a local church because they are mature and their parent organizations encourage church relationships. But it may not be easy to recruit the members of a para-local church group. They do not always identify their para-local church association, nor should they be expected or required to do so. They also have a particular set of expectations and experiences. They range from young people with little church background to mature Christians who received significant growth and ministry opportunities in para-local church groups.

In this chapter, I want to concentrate first on how the local church can relate to the members of para-local church organizations and, second, to the staff of such organizations.

There is no fail-safe method for relating these people to a local congregation. But certain guidelines will help considerably.

RECRUITING AND INTEGRATING PARA-LOCAL CHURCH MEMBERS

Pastor Jerry Mitchell was deeply influenced in his early

twenties by a para-local church organization. He considers this training a big influence in his life. He later went to seminary and now is a highly effective pastor in the Seattle area. He is a strong local church advocate and a strong supporter of para-local church endeavors. As a result, his church has drawn many people trained in para-local church groups and they serve in important positions in the church.

But how can your church attract and integrate para-local church participants?

Be direct on your position. Honesty and forthrightness are always the best approach. Consequently, if your church takes a very negative position on para-local church groups in general, be direct in sharing that position. There is a real temptation to say nothing and try to bring people to your viewpoint, or to recruit them away from para-local church participation and support. Certainly you should discuss the issues with them, but it would be unethical to actively involve them and later precipitate conflict over this issue. Normally such a position results from the belief that para-local church organizations are biblically illegitimate.

Be accepting. One of the hallmarks of a vital church is its acceptance of a person with his needs, hang-ups, and problems, as well as his gifts. We all thrive on personal acceptance. Without it, we shrivel up and die. No one enjoys living under a cloud of suspicion or reservation. So when para-local church members visit or regularly attend your church, encourage them. Stimulate them. Use their gifts. Make them feel needed and accepted. Determine ways to assimilate them and their unique contribution to the body.

However, by acceptance I do not mean unquestioning acceptance of everyone's lifestyle or doctrinal views. This would violate the meaning of a united body of believers. I do mean accepting them as fellow believers and acknowledging the value of their training, background, and gifts.

Acceptance is communicated in a variety of ways. Be creative in the ways you demonstrate your acceptance. You have nothing to lose and much to gain.

"Accept one another, then, just as Christ accepted you, in order to bring praise to God" (Romans 15:7).

Do not push for immediate involvement. Most people do not want to be pushed toward extensive involvement right away. Even more so, people from para-local church organizations may need a period of time to acclimate to your fellowship. Some may be a bit burned out from overcommitment and activity in their para-local church group. They also may still be deeply involved. If you push them too fast, you may lose them. Find out the levels of their commitments and what they would like to do.

Para-local church members will fall into several categories:
1. Young Christians whose only involvement has been a para-local church group.
2. More mature Christians who are disassociating from a para-local church group and moving into the church for their primary fellowship and ministry.
3. Christians who still maintain some active involvement with a para-local church group.

It is imperative to keep these distinctives in mind in order to relate properly to each category.

For young Christians, their association with the church will have been minimal. They know little of its purpose, organization, or function. Even when they have been introduced to the church by para-local church staff, their commitment and understanding will be small. Many come out of a pagan background, and what little church exposure they may have had as non-Christians was a negative experience. Be patient with them. Do not expect them to buy in to the whole church concept. They need time to grow and see the need for the larger body of Christ.

You can involve the more mature Christians faster. They have already decided to change their primary ministry focus from a para-local church ministry to the church. They will have specific gifts and training that will benefit the church significantly. However, they are probably emerging from a fairly intense involvement, so use caution in overloading too quickly. In any case, they need time to demonstrate their loyalty and commitment to the church as a participating member, not just as a leader.

The most difficult people to involve are those in the third category. Their continuing active involvement in both the church and the para-local church puts a strain on their ability to do both well. The church can view them as nonparticipatory, or it can view their ministry as a legitimate extension of the ministries of the church.

Personally, I prefer to see these people carry one major responsibility in the church in addition to their outside ministry. The attitude of the church and its staff makes all the difference. They can be considered missionaries or misfits. It's all a question of how broadly we view the ministry of our local congregation.

Do not be overly critical of "holes" in the person's development. Whether our growth has occurred largely in the church or in a para-local church group, we all have needs and shortcomings. Every church, denomination, and para-local church organization emphasizes particular growth steps for young Christians. Much will be in common; but many areas will be different.

We focus too easily on the teaching shortcomings of others. How much better to be thankful for what has been taught, and to proceed to fill in some of the gaps. No one church or group will meet the total needs of every person. Be tolerant of the gaps the para-local church ministry did not fill.

Also, be tolerant of the young people emerging from involvement in para-local church ministries. They are excited and enthusiastic about what they have learned. They want to share it wherever they go. Yet their experience is so limited that they can be too pushy—or even critical when the church does not meet their expectations.

When I was on the faculty of the Air Force academy, we occasionally had overly zealous young Christians offend a chaplain because he did not meet their set of expectations in preaching or teaching. Then the chaplain might fix the blame on the Navigators or whichever group the young men were involved with.

I remember telling one chaplain, "Please remember that these men are only eighteen or nineteen years old—and that they often act their age. Please don't blame the Navigators for all their actions. If there is a problem call me and let's work it out."

It's a bit like the speech a first grade teacher gave the parents at the beginning of each year. She said, "I'll promise not to believe everything they tell me about you, if you'll promise not to believe everything they tell you about me!"

Be tolerant of their initial attempts to change the church to fit what they think it should be. Make good use of their enthusiasm by channeling it to useful places in the body.

Discover their interests and gifts. Just as you would find out the interests of anyone entering the congregation, so you should discover the interests of para-local church members. In informal sharing times, you will learn much about their background and perceived gifts. Let them know that you want to minister to them as a family, as well as to see them used in the body. As they are drawn into friendships in the body, they will be recruited to the full ministry of the church.

RELATING TO PARA-LOCAL CHURCH STAFF

A series of questions flash through the minds of most pastors when staff of various para-local church ministries come into their fellowship. What is their doctrinal position? Are they here because they want to be here or just for public relations? Do they want financial support? Will they recruit the church leadership to their ministry? Will they be Sunday morning pew-warmers or will they really contribute?

Another set of questions should also capture pastors' minds. What are their personal and family needs? Have they ever had a real church home? How could we integrate their ministry expertise and emphasis into our congregation? Do they need some special encouragement? Do they need personal friendship and acceptance?

Your attitude will determine your outward response toward them. What an encouragement several churches have been to our family over the years. Pastors and church members alike have embraced us as a family and ministered to us in ways they will never know.

Here are some specific steps you can take to be of like encouragement.

Initiate a personal relationship with para-local church staff. You have many questions about them and their organization, and they have many questions about you and your church. Unless answers are provided, the mind will supply its own from comments, impressions, and hearsay. The answers may be totally untrue, but they will fill the mind anyway. Meet fantasy with fact.

Get to know them on a personal basis. You will both benefit. Do not overidentify them with their organization, or what you may have heard about their organization. They are individuals with needs and desires like anyone else. If your church is clearly opposed to para-local church groups, be up front and say so. You may be saving future conflict for both of you.

Pray together. When you interact with para-local church staff, do not just talk philosophy, doctrine, or ministry. Pray together around the throne of grace. Make specific plans to pray for each other and with each other, or it will rarely happen. Schedule it into your week and keep it a priority.

Minister to them and their families. Para-local church staff need the fellowship of the body of Christ like anyone else. Often they are geographically separated from other co-workers and family, and lack real caring fellowship. Normally their ministry specialization does not meet the needs of their children. Draw them into your fellowship and minister to their family needs. Your church can be a place of refuge for them. Remember, too, that they could well have had negative experiences in other congregations. Some need to be encouraged to value the local church's ministry to their family.

Use them in their specialty. Para-local church staff usually possess some characteristics in common. They are highly motivated in a particular type of ministry. They have specific training and gifts to fulfill that ministry. Consequently, we would be wise to use them in their area of expertise and motivation. The range of specialties is broad: evangelism, discipleship, counseling, and missions; working with children, the poor, foreign students, ethnic groups, and women. There are a myriad of others. Take advantage of their training and interest by putting them to work in your local congregation.

Do not make them foundational to your church. Remember that para-local church staff have their own ministries. They will not be able to contribute much more than the mature layman since they have their job to do also. Therefore, do not try to build on them as key foundations of your church. Enable them to do their ministry rather than recruit them to do yours. Certainly they can and should be a vital part of the local body, but they cannot become a functional part of the church staff without jeopardizing the integrity of their own ministry. Because they are trained and talented, it is easy to expect too much of them. Be realisitc in your expectations.

Avoid a competitive posture. Some churches fear that para-local church staff will recruit from their congregations. And this is likely to happen from time to time. People influence people. Insurance salesmen sell insurance, doctors receive patients, car dealers sell cars, and cabinetmakers build cabinets for members of the congregation. No one can avoid who they are or what they do.

So, in all likelihood, para-local church staff will influence some toward their ministry. But isn't that what we want—people in a congregation activating their faith, receiving training, and reaching out? The conflict usually comes when a key layman decides to become involved in a para-local church ministry instead of the one he was doing in the church. That is bound to happen. But we need to broaden the view of our church. Do we only approve of the para-local church ministry outside our church, or do we accept it within also? Usually if para-local church staff influence one or two from the church to colabor with them, many more will have been influenced to do the same type of ministry within the body. Do we rejoice only in our work, or also in the work of others in the body of Christ? Keep communication open on this issue. Clear communication can appease much suspicion and conflict. This is a dual responsibility of the church and para-local church staff.

SOME GENERAL SUGGESTIONS

Relating to para-local church societies is not an easy task for most churches. So many groups have been founded in the past decade that most are virtually unknown to the general Christian public. Pastors are bewildered by the many new groups springing up daily. Perhaps a few general suggestions will help facilitate good relationships and enhance your local church ministry.

Utilize para-local church groups. Instead of fighting para-local church groups, use them to benefit your ministry. They have significant specialties that could be used in your church, on your terms. Invite them to put on a seminar, train some of your leaders, teach a class, or speak in your services. Use them to provide training where you need it to strengthen your programs.

Do not try to duplicate para-local church efforts. Whenever we see a specialist group doing a good job and attracting the attention of our members, we tend to think, "We ought to start a ministry like that in our church." Resist the temptation! Unless your church is quite large, you cannot afford the money or the staff required to do it. Every church cannot produce a quality program in youth, music, outreach to ethnic groups, marriage counseling, production of material for small groups, and so on.

We need to concentrate on what we do well in the church and must continue to do. Bring in temporary specialists for the rest. However, if your church is quite large you may be able to perform some specialized ministries well, such as campus evangelism, ministry to the needy, or ethnic outreach. But even then, make sure it is a real need and not just a response to a current fad. Above all, do not get into a competitive posture with para-local church organizations. Function as a body with each part supplying a needed function whether inside or outside the local congregation.

Do not blame para-local church groups for their problem members. Would you like to be judged as a church by the lives of only two or three of your members—especially if they were chosen at random? Very likely not. People are people, with both strengths and faults. Not every person will be a good testimony for the para-local church group that reached and helped them. They will not always reflect the beliefs and interests of the organization. And often a person will identify with a para-local church ministry when they actually received only minor help from them. If you have questions, go to the source—a staff person or the headquarters of the para-local church group.

Do not lump all para-local church organizations together. Churches are different. Some good, some not so good. Some effective, some not so effective. Some in doctrinal agreement with us, some in disagreement. So it is with para-local church organizations. They are as different as churches are different. We often see people abandoning or blaming the church after only one visit or one bad experience in the past. We think, "If only they would give us a try. We are different."

Extend the same courtesy to the para-local church groups you encounter. Some are effective, some ineffective. Some coincide with your beliefs, some don't. Simply trust them individually as you would wish your church to be trusted. Isn't there a verse that says about the same thing? "Do to others as you would have them do to you" (Luke 6:31).

Do not project faults of individual para-local church staff to the whole organization. Often the leadership of a para-local church society is more mature and moderate than some of their field staff. I know of one pastor who had a conflict with a para-local church staff person about thirty years ago. To this day, it is still in his mind and affects his view of the whole organization. We must allow for change and growth both as individuals and as groups.

We also need to realize that a staff person (especially the younger ones) may not represent fully the position or spirit of the entire organization. Recognize the individuality of each para-local church staff person. Of course, there is always the possibility that they *do* represent the position and attitude of the parent organization. At least make a genuine attempt to discover which is the case.

You need not support all para-local church groups. Blanket approval of all para-local church ministries is no more logical than blanket approval of all local churches. Because you financially support or approve of one does not obligate you to endorse another. Each group, like each local church, has its distinctives and its specialties. Each church should pick and choose its associations. Judge each group on its individual merits.

"And let us consider how we may spur one another on toward love and good deeds. Let us not give up meeting together, as some are in the habit of doing, but let us encourage one another—and all the more as you see the Day approaching."
Hebrews 10:24-25

Chapter 8

Handbook for the Para-Local Church

*T*he illustration at the beginning of the previous chapter could be reversed. The cold handshake and the wariness could easily have been shown by the para-local church staff person. Not everyone has a high view of the local church. In all likelihood, the staff person has had some bad experience with the local church in the past. Also, a pastor will quickly recognize an attitude of superiority or distrust. If one attends a local church simply out of obligation or in response to organizational policy, this will soon become apparent.

One para-local church staff family moved to a smaller city where evangelical churches were not plentiful. They began attending one, but never joined. The church encountered some problems, and they left and visited another. After five years they still had not committed themselves to a church. Some Sundays they would not even be in the worship service, although they were in the city. Obviously, they had little influence in the community of Christians and bore a negative testimony for their organization—not to mention the significant blessing they lost as a family.

Strained relationships are not always the fault of the local church. Many times para-local church staff precipitate problems by how *they* relate. Some may communicate that they have little need for the local church. Some can be so intent on their mission that they become insensitive. Others may transmit a proud manner about their unique contribution. Sometimes younger, less experienced staff do not have the maturity for smooth interrelationships with local churches.

People who don't have children over the ages of four or five often do not see the need for a local fellowship as much as they will later—especially when they have teenagers. These people can be quite self-sufficient in their younger adult years. Later they will have a much greater appreciation for the entire body of Christ. They will discover that the local church gives broader support, encouragement, training, teaching, and opportunities for ministry. Para-local church leaders can do much to help their staff early in their careers to understand and appreciate the local church.

Tony and Cheryl Naff served as staff of a para-local church society in a small college town. They fellowshiped in a local church regularly and were involved in a small group fellowship within the church. When, in the sovereignty of God, their second child was stillborn, the importance of the local church became evident. Their fellow staff were supportive and helpful, but did not live in the same city. It was the people in the church who immediately got behind them, bringing meals, encouraging, giving money, and lifting their load. Through this trauma they saw the local body at work. Though they were involved earlier, through this incident their appreciation of the local church grew immensely. "We saw them help us in a way that our fellow staff couldn't—even though they wanted to. We really became believers in the local body."

IMPROVING ORGANIZATIONAL RELATIONSHIPS
WITH THE LOCAL CHURCH

Para-local church organizations can do much to foster good relationships and interdependence. Here are some suggestions.

Clarify your mission and vision. Any para-local church organization needs to define its ministry. This should be reflected in both organizational and public communication. Para-local church staff need to understand and agree with the vision and mission as it relates to their local ministry. In turn, they need to be skilled in communicating their vision and mission to pastors and others.

After an organization has been in existence for a number of years, it will need to reclarify its mission. Has it changed? Are the staff still unified around this mission and contributing to it in their day-to-day work? Is the organization still needed? What are its distinctives? Its strengths? Its weaknesses? These questions will help sharpen the focus of the para-local church contribution.

Define your relationship to local churches. Much confusion results when staff do not understand their organization's relationship to local churches. This relationship will largely be determined by the vision and mission of the organization. Some will focus on direct contribution to local churches. Others will concentrate on ministry quite apart from a local church.

It is wise to differentiate between the organization's relationship to the local church, and a staff person's individual or family relationship to a church. The former is a function of the mission. The latter is a practical matter relating to the welfare of the staff person. Without such a distinction, a staff person can become sidetracked from his specialist calling and become overinvolved with a local church. If direct involvement with the local church is part of his assigned mission, then that could be acceptable. But in general, a para-local church society is not a supplier of staff for a local church.

Para-local church staff need to understand this distinction and be instrumental in communicating it to their local churches. Even groups that focus on church renewal or church equipping must exercise caution to maintain their special contribution to the local church.

Additionally, para-local church leaders need to clarify what their desires are for their members' future local church involvement. If they want their members to eventually be involved in the local church, they must help them make that transition. It is too easy to assume they will manage the transition on their own. No doubt they have received counsel from para-local church staff on other issues, so why not on this one? Conserving for a lifetime the fruit of a para-local church ministry ought to be a prime desire of any group.

Develop a brief doctrinal statement. Almost every local church wants to know where a para-local church organization stands doctrinally. The more lengthy and detailed the statement, the more narrow the local church constituency will become. The more brief and broad the statement, the broader the relationships to local churches can be. On the other hand, some churches will not be supportive because they do not see their personal doctrinal distinctives clearly spelled out in the para-local church statement.

Issues that should be included are the view of Scripture, the deity of Christ, and the doctrine of salvation. These are the core concerns of most evangelical churches. Developing a doctrinal statement will also help an organization clarify its own thinking theologically.

A valid criticism by many pastors is that para-local church groups are weak on their doctrinal view. Do you have doctrinal boundaries that no staff member can step over without disqualifying himself for service in your organization? Simply being conservative and evangelical will not prevent personal doctrinal error in your next generation of staff.

Develop consistent communication with local churches. Many para-local church groups fall under suspicion simply because no one knows what they do or do not believe. Silence is deadly. Establish means of communication with local churches either through printed material or personal contacts. The larger the organization the more crucial this communication becomes.

Perhaps para-local church groups need to develop a special pastor's packet that provides more information than individual staff would normally communicate. Key pastors make an excellent source of counsel. Their input and advice is valuable not only for help and suggestions, but for recruiting financial support and for public relations.

Do not try to be all things to all churches. It is virtually impossible for para-local church groups to please all local churches. Almost any organization will have distinctives or doctrines that draw them to one type of local church and separate them from others. Para-local church groups must maintain their organizational distinctives rather than compromise to please a special segment of churches. Some irritants can be removed, but mission and calling must supercede public relations.

This may mean that some local churches will not support certain para-local church groups. But those churches are probably not the ones who will support para-local church groups anyway, since there will always be some areas of disagreement. For instance, some organizations do not take a stand on political issues. This irritates some churches that are strongly outspoken on public issues. However, such a policy may open doors to other churches. The key is not to compromise the calling to please a few people.

IMPROVING INDIVIDUAL STAFF RELATIONSHIPS WITH THE LOCAL CHURCH

Whereas the previous suggestions apply mainly to para-local church *organizations*, the following apply to *individual staff* of those organizations.

Be a functioning part of a local church. One of my close friends and co-workers, Paul Drake, retired from the Marine Corps and began serving full-time in a ministry to the military. In a military ministry, it is easy just to attend an interdenominational chapel and not have a deep, personal relationship with a local congregation. Paul didn't do this. He became a vital part of a local church while still performing his assigned ministry. After some time, his stature in the community was such that he was selected Executive Director of the San Diego Evangelical Association—an association of churches whose board is primarily pastors. He knew how to balance his para-local church ministry and his personal relationship to the local church.

As you unite with a local congregation, it is important to do so out of your own convictions and needs. You must also remember that you publically represent your organization, and your actions and attitudes reflect directly on your parent group. Several principles facilitate relationships with local churches.

1. Base your selection of a local church on the needs of your family and on your doctrinal position. You are the only one who can determine these needs. You may be tempted to go to a church that is the best for public relations, but does not give you or your family the kind of encouragement and ministry you need. The placement of your church membership is a critical decision and should be the subject of much prayer. It is traumatic to have to leave a church because you did not choose well at the beginning. In seeking the right church I suggest you consider the following:

- Doctrinal compatibility
- Positive attitudes toward para-local church groups (and your group in particular)
- Size (particularly as it relates to your children's needs)
- Stage of the church (new, in a building program, well-established, recovering from a split)
- Public preaching and teaching ministry
- Expectations of its members
- Counsel of those who know the church

2. Attempt to develop friendships with the pastor and church staff. A personal relationship provides a foundation from which many future problems or conflicts can be resolved. Use pastoral staff for personal counsel and for encouragement in your work.

We have found personal friendships with our pastors to be lifelong relationships. I recall one pastor who, upon not seeing me in the service (although I was there), prayed, "Bless Jerry White as he is ministering elsewhere today." There was the mutual trust that if I was not there, it was for a good reason. Becoming friends as couples brings an added dimension to the relationship. Such a friendship may not always be possible, especially in a large church or if your age difference is great. Don't push it, but make yourself available. (For specific help on developing pastoral friendships, see chapter 10 of *Friends and Friendship: The Secrets of Drawing Closer.*[1])

3. Contribute in a specific way to the ministry of the church. Take a responsibility and do it well. Use your skills and ministry focus to make a contribution where feasible within your local church. Be cautious not to become so overcommitted that conflict develops with fulfilling your primary ministry.

I have always enjoyed the opportunity to teach a class periodically even though my travel schedule makes for irregular attendance at my local church. I have found pastors to be very understanding of my circumstances, and willing to use me when I am available. My wife, Mary, has generally been involved in music and a committee responsibility as well. In addition, we did our part in the nursery schedule as the children were growing up. We have great memories and friendships from our involvements.

4. Be accountable to a local church for your personal and family life. Some may feel that their personal accountability should be to their staff supervisor. Certainly it can be to some extent. But who sees you weekly in your family and marriage relationship? Who knows your reputation in the community? Who sees your children in action and knows how you are caring for them? Most often it will be your church.

Accountability for your para-local church ministry, however, rests with your parent organization. Do not confuse personal and ministry responsibility. The authority for your primary ministry must reside with your direct supervisor. Use your pastor and others for counsel and help, but be responsible to your own organization.

5. Be regular in attendance at your local church. Be loyal to the ministry of your local congregation. If you must be absent, let them know what you are doing both for their prayer support and to prevent misunderstandings.

One para-local church staff person felt he had been ministering all week, so Sunday was his "day off" and he didn't go to church. You can imagine his reputation in the community. What is more critical is that he harbored a serious misconception of the meaning of ministry, and his need for that kind of fellowship.

Select a church that agrees with your ministry. As you become a part of a local church, you will want them to approve of your ministry. Being part of a local church where a silent (or spoken) disapproval hangs over your head does not help you, nor does it help the church.

The key to a church's attitude is its pastor. Therefore, an honest conversation with the pastor is crucial when selecting your church. Do not expect full agreement from him. He may ask direct questions about your ministry. Sense his spirit toward your work, and let him sense yours toward the church. Acceptance is a two-way street.

You will need to prove yourself as a part of that congregation over a period of time, especially if you are with a relatively unknown or small group. Let time and your performance demonstrate that your ministry deserves their support (and this support need not be financial). It is a positive sign when your church does decide to support you financially, but it is not requisite for joining.

Do not try to reform your church. As you relate to your local church, do not try to change everything to your way of thinking. Certainly you should be an influence by your life and personal example, but you should not expect your local church to adopt every aspect of your personal ministry emphasis. In relating to other churches and pastors, learn to be sensitive to their needs and their church situations. Be a servant to the local church, not a reformer.

I recognize that some para-local church agencies have church renewal as their aim, but even that aim must proceed with wisdom and patience—and in full cooperation with pastoral staff.

When you are a part of a local church, be a contributing part, not a thorn in its side. And as you participate, do not abandon the church when things do not please you. Do not be a church hopper.

Direct the fruit of your ministry into the local congregation. As you minister in your specialty, be a positive influence for the local church to those you help. Avoid being critical of local churches or other organizations. Criticism never helps. It usually backfires and increases the tension. Encourage those in your ministry, especially new believers, to be a part of a local fellowship. This will be a perfectly natural involvement as they observe your example.

I recall attending a church in a university town while I was in graduate school. I was also on the lay staff of the Navigators. I selected a church that met our family needs and did not insist that the students I was helping attend with us. However, it was not long before these students filled about one-fourth of this small church. They attended simply because I did. This resulted in a more significant testimony to the pastor than all the talking I ever could have done.

Learn to communicate your mission and ministry well. You need to have clear, personal conviction about your ministry in order to communicate it well. No ministry is just a job—it is a calling. But even a clear calling needs clear communication. As you raise finances and prayer support, people need to understand your ministry. As you relate to pastors, you will need to communicate this calling frequently. Unclear communication gives the impression of a fuzzy understanding of your own work. In your own church, make certain the pastor and key people know what you *really* do.

Keep your own focus clear. You must not lose sight of your own task. Many para-local church staff have significant freedom in their use of time. You can easily be drawn into other good ministries in your local church and neglect the ministry you were called to do as a para-local church staff. If this occurs, much conflict will result with your pastor and with your supervisor as you are pressed to realign your emphasis. For a clear conscience, be sure that you really give a full measure of work to your assigned task.

Since writing does not fall within the direct responsibilities of my ministry job, I became concerned that I might be robbing time from my job in order to write. Consequently, about three years ago I began keeping records of the amount of time I was spending on my job. This was a great help because I could then see objectively that I was putting in fifty or more hours a week on my ministry responsibilities. That time did not include my local church involvements or time spent in writing.

Beyond all these suggestions, *keep a godly attitude* toward the ministry of the local church and toward other works. Being convinced of your vision is not to be prideful about it. "Humble yourselves, therefore, under God's mighty hand, that he may lift you up in due time" (1 Peter 5:6). You are a significant part of the body and work of Christ, but only a part. The body must function in harmony—not always doing the same thing in unison, but in harmony—each giving honor to the other.

Chapter 8, Notes

1. Jerry and Mary White, *Friends and Friendship: The Secrets of Drawing Closer* (Colorado Springs: Navpress, 1982), pp. 143f.

"From Attalia they sailed back to Antioch, where they had been committed to the grace of God for the work they had now completed. On arriving there, they gathered the church together and reported all that God had done through them and how he had opened the door of faith to the Gentiles."
Acts 14:26-27

Chapter 9

Handbook for Participants in the Para-Local Church

*T*ransition and change are never easy. Changing to a new church after a move to a new city is difficult. Few churches ever measure up to the last one, especially at first glance. Expectations are high and built on past experience.

My wife and I interacted over dinner one Sunday with a couple who were trying to find a church after a recent move to a new city. They had tried a church that many people raved about, but in our conversation they consistently criticized the new church and praised their former one. The relationships, the experiences, the pastor, and the fellowship consumed their memories and colored their view. They will never find a church like their former one. And if they returned to it in three years, it would not satisfy them either, for it too would have changed.

No change is easy. And the transition from the warm, small group atmosphere of many para-local church groups to a local church is no less easy. But unless the para-local church group changes its focus and decides to start a church, the transition must be made. Even if a para-local church group decides to plant a church, it will soon lose the distinctives and focus that were its hallmark as a para-local church organization.

Most former members of para-local church societies will

eventually flow to some local church. Seldom do para-local church people boycott the organized church to stay within a small fellowship. When that has occurred, a new church inevitably results or the group finally disintegrates.

Alan was an enthusiastic young man with a vision to reach out to people. He had been trained in a para-local church context and was now launching out on his own. He and his family moved to take a job in a new city, and they began to look for a church. They found a fine church where the pastor welcomed them warmly. In fact, the pastor seemed to have a vision similar to Alan's. The pastor encouraged him to share his vision with the laymen of the church. But things did not move as fast as Alan desired. He became impatient. The church was going through some internal trauma of which he was not aware. Soon he confronted the pastor with his "lack of integrity" in what he had "promised" Alan. He accused the pastor before the board. Needless to say, he had to leave the church. All this occurred within a two month period. Here was a man who did not know how to earn his right to be heard.

Many problems make the transition difficult. People who were converted out of a nonreligious context take considerable time to appreciate and integrate into the church system, or even to fellowship at an informal group level. They are not like puppies who automatically know where to go for milk. They have no sudden "warm feelings" for organ music, the great hymns, and a well-dressed congregation sitting in rows and standing on command to sing or pray. The forms are totally foreign to them.

The days are past when we could assume that most people attended church as children. People from nonevangelical churches do not automatically feel comfortable with gospel messages, verse-by-verse exposition, or an altar call, even though they have made a sincere commitment to Christ. If you want to understand this feeling, visit a church at the opposite end of the spectrum from yours. You will feel distinctly uncomfortable as you attempt to follow the pattern of service and blend in with the congregation. Just so, new Christians will experience discomfort as they enter a new church.

This chapter will consider two categories of para-local church members. The first is those who are effectively leaving a para-local church group environment and are transitioning into the local church. They will have little intense involvement with the para-local church organization in the future. This is often the case with people leaving student or military ministries. The second category includes people either entering a local church or already in it, but who will continue to have an active involvement with the para-local church organization. Although I will initially address the first category, in many ways the suggestions will be applicable to both.

SUGGESTIONS FOR THOSE FORMERLY INVOLVED
IN THE PARA-LOCAL CHURCH

Do not expect the same relationship and help from the local church. The local church cannot be a duplicate of the group you came from. Both its purpose and its structure are different. No doubt your para-local church group was small or individually oriented with a high sense of identification. This can happen in the local church also, but it will take time to develop those relationships. It is easy to forget how slowly you integrated into the previous group.

The local church ministers to a broad segment of people and not everything will meet your specific needs. You will be developed in new areas of your life. Be thankful for the training and help you have had, but be open to new input and new ideas. Your para-local church group probably drew you in on a personal level through friends in your dormitory, class, or neighborhood. In a sense you were in an incubator where input was geared to your specific needs. Now you have grown and been equipped to relate in the larger world of believers. (I almost said, "The cold, cruel world!" I trust this is not the picture of the local church.) As you enter another environment as a stranger with no sponsor or friend, you need to lower, change, and broaden your expectations.

Select a local church that fits you. If you are like many young Christians, you may have no experience with a local church.

Perhaps you attended with the staff person of the para-local church group or with others involved with you. Recall the key characteristics of the preaching, atmosphere, and doctrine. Seek out a similar church, possibly one from the same denomination or with a similar structure.

When moving to a new area, ask people you trust for recommendations or attend with them. When we moved to Seattle in 1978, we hardly shopped at all for a church. My wife's brother had selected a church a few years previously, and we knew his doctrine and taste would be much like ours. So we settled in quickly, though not without conversation with the pastor. It was an excellent decision for us and we were not disappointed.

When I suggest a church that fits you, I mean one that fits you doctrinally, socially, and structurally. There are no perfect fits, but the church you choose should be one where you will not always be uncomfortable or in disagreement. When you are selecting, attend more than the morning service. The life of the church will be more apparent in the Sunday evening services or the Sunday school classes. Consider the church as a whole, not just the morning worship service.

As a young Christian and newly commissioned Air Force officer, I took Mary and went looking for a church in a town where we did not know a single person. On Sunday evening we drove around the small southern town looking for a church that held an evening service. We thought surely it must be a good church if it had two services on Sunday! (You can tell how mature my understanding was then.) We found one, went in, and were warmly received. They even asked me to lead in prayer in the service. I told the pastor that I was not a member of their denomination, and the prayer offer was quickly withdrawn. I sensed something strange in the service. I had no knowledge of the denomination, but when the pastor later called on us, I realized they were doctrinally unsound in their understanding of salvation. Needless to say, we did not return. We later found a large church where the minister of music befriended us and drew us in. We were both young and vulnerable, but fortunately had enough doctrinal background to detect error.

Come in to serve and learn. Bob and Judy Neal are friends of ours who have a vision for discipling and evangelism. Bob's early training was with a para-local church group. During a five-year military career, they both reached out effectively to people around them, convinced that God had called them to minister as lay people. When they left the military, they moved to a city and began fellowshiping in a local church. They came in softly and began to serve. They did not push the church to adopt their particular vision. Soon they became leaders in the church. Bob recently became an elder and now has a significant influence in discipling and evangelism. They still maintain involvement in a para-local church group, but balance it well with their church responsibility. He has earned the right to be heard, and now can use his earlier training to its maximum.

As you enter a new church, be patient in your acceptance and involvement. On the other hand, don't be silent about your para-local church background—pastors and others need to know about that. Unfortunately, people are often so silent about their training and background that pastoral staff do not realize where they were helped in their salvation or growth.

Do not push for immediate involvement. If you are a young person from a student ministry, you were probably a leader in that group. As an aggressive young person you may come in wanting to teach a class or be assigned a place of leadership. The Christian education pastor rejoices and offers you a third grade boys class, whereas you may have had in mind an adult class or at least the college class. But a church is naturally reluctant to assign a key adult class to someone in their early to mid twenties. You will need to earn your right to teach and be an influence in the local church. Develop a serving attitude and there will always be a place for you. Be willing to wait.

Give the church a fair opportunity to prove itself. Do not be a church hopper. I have seen too many people leave a church after only a brief stay. They discover something wrong and head down the road to find the perfect church. They never will. Usually they go from church to church and make no significant contribution anywhere. I suggest a minimum of two years (after your initial few weeks of screening) to integrate into the body of a local church.

While ministering recently in another church in our area, I saw someone I knew come into the service. They had previously attended our church (for the second time), but had left it for another one. Now they had moved again, all within a space of four years. Some people have a difficult time settling into a church and making a consistent contribution.

Give financially to the local church. The principle of Galatians 6:6 is to give to those who minister to you. You probably have financial commitments to the para-local church group with which you were involved. Keep those commitments, but not to the exclusion of your local church. Learn to increase your giving year by year, and to give sacrificially. Where you put your money is where your heart will be.

Be faithful in the local church. Faithfulness to the functions of the church is key to acceptance. Recall the demands and expectations of your para-local church involvement. They probably encouraged you to attend every function of the group. Pastors feel the same way. They have certain expectations for people who are loyal to the local body. Most churches simply do not respect people whose only involvement is the Sunday morning worship service. And regularity is important. "Let us not give up meeting together, as some are in the habit of doing, . . ." (Hebrews 10:25). Loyalty and dependability are key character traits of mature believers. Your presence is also an influence on others.

Suggestions for Those Presently Involved in the Para-Local Church

The relational dynamics change considerably for the person who desires involvement in *both* local church and para-local church structures. Conflict will arise. My suggestions here apply primarily to adults with dual involvement, not to students at the college level. Collegiate para-local church groups function almost as a de facto student church because of the totality of their involvement together in the unique student environment. Students should certainly attend and be introduced to a local church fellowship, but they cannot handle full involvement in both structures. The training and intense help they receive on the campus will greatly benefit the local church at a later time.

Keep your pastor well-informed. When you are highly involved in a para-local church ministry outside your local church, you need to make an extra effort to keep your pastor informed of what you are doing and of your leading from the Lord. Ask for prayer and personal encouragement. The pastor needs to know that you are not avoiding work in the local context, but are being productive as an extension of your local church.

Do not abandon all local church responsibilities. Involvement in a para-local church ministry should not replace involvement in a church. Most people can still handle one responsibility in a local fellowship, since they will usually be involved in the life of the church as a family. And whatever you do, do it well.

Gauge your capacity and avoid overcommitment. Everyone has a different capacity for activity and pressure. It varies with age and family circumstances, as well as your personal gifting from God. Some people can keep many things going at one time, while others feel pressured doing only one church responsibility. Each of us has only so much time and capacity. If you are a low-capacity person, avoid attempting a significant, regular dual involvement. Put your major efforts in the local church. You can still remain peripherally involved with your para-local church group in special events and irregular contact, as well as giving. A high-capacity person, or one whose employment or job is flexible, can handle both involvements and should use his capacity to the fullest.

Do not expect instantaneous acceptance. Whether you are just entering a church or have been in one for some time, do not expect the local church to accept your para-local church involvement unreservedly or quickly. Obviously, you are a potential worker in that local church. But outside involvement limits your availability. Even if your pastor approves of the para-local church, you can hardly blame him for making his bid for your involvement in the local church structure. You will need to demonstrate your continuing loyalty to the local church as you pursue ministry outside it.

Do not expect your distinctive ministry to be needed in your local church. Everyone has their hobbyhorse and pet emphasis. Whether it is small groups, evangelism, care units, social concerns, music, youth, discipleship, Bible studies, or any number of other good things, the local church cannot do all of them at once. Nor do they always have that special need.

Consequently, you cannot always expect to pursue the distinctive skills and vision you learned in a para-local church group. Not only are there many good emphases, but there are several ways of approaching each one. Though your strength may be evangelism, the church may already be involved in an evangelism program that is different than one you would prefer. Be willing to wait until your emphasis is needed.

Guard against an attitude of superiority. One danger of a specialist skill or ministry is pride. We all agree that such an attitude is sin, but it can still creep in almost undetected by our own perception. Others will see it. We must value every part of the body and affirm their contributions. No one person or group ever has a monopoly on spirituality, skills, or ministry methods. The local church, as a generalist structure, will always have some weakness, but we must never regard any other part of the body of Christ as inferior. "For who makes you different from anyone else? What do you have that you did not receive? And if you did receive it, why do you boast as though you did not?" (1 Corinthians 4:7).

One final comment is needed. Even though you are not an official representative of a para-local church society, you cannot help having a profound effect on the attitude of the local church toward that society. How you relate to a local church will have an effect on their view of your specific para-local church group. No matter how a group communicates their policy regarding local church relations, no policy will speak as loudly as the actions of people like yourself. You can be the glue in joining the breach between the local church and the para-local church.

"Now all has been heard;
here is the conclusion of the matter:
Fear God and keep his commandments,
for this is the whole duty of man.
For God will bring every deed into judgment,
including every hidden thing,
whether it is good or evil."
Ecclesiastes 12:13-14

Conclusion

A Final Plea

E vangelical Christianity is a broken society with conflict, infighting, and competition rivaling that of the industrial world. These battles have no bullets and bombs, but forces of pride, criticism, and suspicion destroy just as completely. As we approach one minute to midnight on the infamous doomsday clock, how dare we turn inward to claw at our own sores when the world is dying without Christ?

We need not resort to an ecumenical alliance with liberal or secular religions. But evangelical local churches and para-local church groups need to labor together and encourage one another to accomplish their best for the kingdom of God. Doctrinal nitpicking, isolationism, and parochial interests cripple us and prevent us from applying our energies toward the task Jesus set before us.

> Then Jesus came to them and said, "All authority in heaven and on earth has been given to me. Therefore go and make disciples of all nations, baptizing them in the name of the Father and of the Son and of the Holy Spirit, and teaching them to obey everything I have commanded you. And surely I will be with you always, to the very end of the age" (Matthew 28:18-20).

When he saw the crowds, he had compassion on
them, because they were harassed and helpless, like
sheep without a shepherd. Then he said to his disciples,
"The harvest is plentiful but the workers are few. Ask
the Lord of the harvest, therefore, to send out workers
into his harvest field" (Matthew 9:36-38).

The task is so great and the laborers so few. The great commission still stands as an imperative to all believers, both corpo-
rately and individually. Each generation has its world to reach with
the gospel. That world is getting larger daily. The population explosion is outstripping our ability to expand and reach out. We
need to reach out in every way we possibly can.

New methods, new vehicles, and new concepts all can fit
with the same gospel. We change the means, not the message. But
above all, we need people to bring the message.

"Everyone who calls on the name of the Lord will be
saved."
How, then, can they call on the one they have not believed in? And how can they believe in the one of whom
they have not heard? And how can they hear without
someone preaching to them? And how can they preach
unless they are sent? (Romans 10:13-15).

God uses people to reach other people. But where are the
people? They are in the church, but they need to be equipped,
mobilized, and sent.

How can we do this? The current structure of the local church
cannot handle the needed rapid expansion, either financially or
structurally. In many ways the para-local church is picking up the
slack. In missionary sending, the independent para-local church
societies are leading the way. As more countries are closing to missionaries, missions thinking has to be revised to include the layman
in his secular profession as the means for entry. Again, para-local
church agencies are taking the lead in this innovation. But we cannot stop here. We must combine to meet the changing situation in
our own country and around the world.

As we mobilize to reach out, our concern must be the building up of the body of Christ, the universal church, not who gets the credit. "In the technical sense, the church has no partners. All of us, church and parachurch, are members of one body serving Jesus Christ and serving his body, the church."[1] But as Scripture and history tell us, the Holy Spirit will not be bound by any human structure to get the gospel message out. When the arteries of the structure become clogged, a new structure will bypass it, taking the form of another local church or a para-local church society. God will not be bound by our forms.

It seems that one of the goals of world evangelization should be to get more people doing more ministry more of the time. The "more people" must involve the equipping and sending of the laity. Yes, sending, not just building them up. But systems for sending by a local church are largely restricted by a formal schooling requirement. Para-local church groups have consistently broken through this barrier by equipping and sending the "unlearned and uneducated" to minister full-time. We still need full-time people. But our current formal educational systems are only a part of the preparation. The New Testament pattern is more "learning by doing."

If local churches do not devise means of equipping and sending lay people, or of accepting the para-local church as a full partner in the body, the proliferation of para-local church societies and ministries will continue. But if the breach can be closed between the local church and the para-local church, then I believe the proliferation of new organizations will decrease as local churches guide people into specific para-local church ministries that have proven productive and reliable. They will also use more laymen full-time on church staffs and in semi-autonomous outreaches in the community.

Another aspect of the place of the para-local church in God's plan is expressed by George Peters, a strong local church advocate.

> There is, however, another aspect to the presence of parachurch organizations. They may exist for a higher purpose. The Holy Spirit may call them into being to

express practically and cross-denominationally the unity of the church of Jesus Christ. He may desire to demonstrate before the world the supra-denominational oneness of the character of the church of God. He may wish to visibly portray the people of God working together in love in the purpose of God. Such possibility must not be discounted.[2]

I do see some danger in the future of the local church and the para-local church. While there is every reason to expect relations to improve and the cause of Christ to advance, pitfalls do exist.

First, if the next few years do not result in greater understanding and acceptance between the two structures, a wider gap could develop. In such a case, members of the para-local church would flow to the few churches who *were* accepting and supportive.

Second, the result of a widening split would almost certainly result in a proliferation of more denomination-like alliances as new churches are formed by members and former members of para-local church groups.

Third, if the gap widens we could see a return to some of the antichurch stance of many in the 1930s. This would be a very unfortunate direction since so much progress has been made in recent years.

Finally, increasing economic downturns on a worldwide basis could make donor competition resemble a business. A crisis could also be precipitated by a significant change in our nation's tax structure. Both local churches and para-local church groups would be hard hit by the elimination of tax deductions for charitable gifts. The local church would be the great loser if property tax exemptions were withdrawn. Neither of these are biblical issues, but both would significantly increase the financial pressures and the conflict.

We must do all we can to draw the two structures together in heart and spirit. On the other hand, we must avoid new interorganizational structures that are doomed to break down by the weight of the impossible task of joining diverse visions and goals. Also, the Roman Catholic process of establishing new orders under the same authority is not a good option. The bond must be spiritual, not structural.

It is my prayer that when history looks back on the last few decades of the twentieth century, it will record a time of great revival in the church and great outreach to the world as evangelical Christianity puts its energies into encouraging rather than competing against one another.

These are exciting times in the body of Christ. Opportunities abound. We need to channel all our energies to meet them. It is obvious that God's hand is on both the local church and the para-local church. Let us do all we can to heal any breach between the two structures, and to thrust out more laborers into the harvest.

Conclusion, Notes

1. George Sweeting, "First, the Good News," *United Evangelical Action*, Fall 1981, pp. 16-18.

2. George W. Peters, *A Theology of Church Growth* (Grand Rapids: Zondervan Publishing House, 1981), pp. 174-75.

Appendix A

The Electronic Church

Several items have not been addressed fully in this study since they relate more to specific issues. These would include an analysis of distinctives between types of para-local church groups, the validity of denominational structures, missions versus home societies, and the so-called electronic church. Because of its high visibility and growing controversy, a few comments on the electronic church are in order.

In the last century, the technological development that had the greatest impact on the local church was the automobile. As the automobile became more common and economical, the local church ceased to be geographically local. Suddenly, people could pick and choose their church more easily. The car gave birth to the superchurches of today. We have adjusted our thinking and programs to this reality to such an extent that the car is rarely even mentioned as a factor.

The next technological development that is just now impacting our society to the fullest is television. The electronic church has been with us for decades on the radio. But its real emotional impact did not arrive until color television invaded the majority of homes. Much has been written about the impact of the communications revolution on our society, but the body of Christ is just now sensing its effect.

Only when a few major programs with a high level of professionalism developed did we begin to hear comments of concern. To this point, radio had become a major way of outreach to peoples around the world. Almost every large church broadcast its morning service and felt it was reaching out to the community. Some even broadcast by television. Also, many radio broadcasts by local pastors were nationwide in their outreach.

But somehow the visual presence of these newer programs has created a greater emotional stir—especially when they request finances. Is there really a significant difference in these forms? They are all a variation of a para-local church effort as it significantly affects thousands of lives. Add to this today's extensive tape ministries of leading pastors, and the picture becomes more complex. Certainly television is a totally inadequate substitute for the personal dynamic of a local congregation. But so are radio programs and "tape churches." On one hand we bless our technology and use it for our advantage, and on the other, we curse its results when they cross some invisible line in our value systems. I do not know the ultimate answer to the place of religious television programs, but we need to be consistent in our view by applying it to the whole of the radio-television-cassette ministries, including those of specific local churches.

The discussion above illustrates our difficulty in maintaining consistency in our views. Theology usually gives way to emotions when finances and people are concerned. Most ministries are acceptable until they begin to have an adverse effect on our particular ministry. As humans it is only natural, though not right, to respond in that way.

Appendix B

Suggested Reasons for the Proliferation of Para-Local Church Groups

*I*n the surveys from pastors, many excellent comments were made about the reasons for the proliferation of para-local church organizations. I believe their insights are worth repeating here. The list contains both direct quotes and summary statements from the surveys. Occasionally, several quotes are grouped together by subject.

1. "Dead orthodoxy in the mainline churches."

"The gross failure of the organized church to function in life and death has caused many to reach for something fresh and vibrant."

"Deterioration and lethargy in many local churches."

"The local church not doing its job, which is tied in with incomplete seminary training."

2. "Preoccupation by many denominations with issues other than personal relationship with Christ and a significant daily walk."

3. "Lack of practical ways of communicating the 'how to's' of the Christian life."

4. "Too tight a structure in churches."

"Failure of churches in broadening their ministries."

"Failure of local churches to band together to effectively meet broad areas of felt need."

5. "An independent spirit."

". . . human egos and fleshly desires *may* be behind some parachurch organizations (and local churches!)."

"Independence and lack of commitment. Our society is overwhelmed by humanism. 'I am it' and if 'I' don't find exactly what 'I' want in the local church, 'I' will start something that will. Best of intentions but wrong motive."

"Many individuals wanting to do their own thing without any accountability."

6. "The realization of needs going unmet."

"Individuals seeing real needs and organizing to meet the specific recognized need. I feel many of these needs would/will exist and continue to appear no matter how well the local church does its job. The work is great and extremely broad."

"Recognized needs that can be better met by an organization that is specialized and has greater resources then a small struggling local church."

7. "Diversity of gifts and a sense of vision on the part of the prime movers in these organizations."

"Local churches under a hundred people do not have trained people to do all that can be done."

"They are doing in a concentrated manner with special talent and interest what most local churches cannot do alone."

8. "Because of lack of cooperation, historically, between them."

"Local churches [that are] only concerned with their own congregations and neighborhoods."

9. "Perhaps the Holy Spirit saying 'separate unto me these people to do this work!' "

"The Lord raising up the parachurch groups."

10. "Most 'achiever-leaders' reason the church is *too slow* to meet the needs; hence a new organization is born to get the job done. We're fortunate that Joshua and Caleb didn't have that mentality centuries ago!"

"An impatience with a lack of [productive ministry] in the church as a whole in each local setting. Some of this impatience is not so noble, however, in that parachurch groups are not making the socio-cultural adaptation necessary to work with, for example, different age groups at different educational levels."

"An unwillingness to work through the constraints of the church."

11. "A drive for productive ministry using biblical principles."

12. "Teaching of both pastors and churches that *pastors* must head up all church ministries."

Appendix C

Sample Surveys

Name: _____ Position: _____

Church: _____

# of Years in Ministry: _____ Church Size: _____

Denomination/Association: _____

Address: _____

For the purpose of this survey, please exclude the "electronic church" (radio, television, etc.), in your answers, except for the one specific question, number 17.

1. Does your church support any parachurch staff or organizations?   ☐ Yes   ☐ No

2. Do you believe that parachurch organizations are
   ☐ Biblical   ☐ Unbiblical   ☐ Neither?

3. Parachurch staff you have *personally* known have been
   ☐ productive members of a local congregation
   ☐ not involved in a local congregation
   ☐ weakly involved in a local congregation

4. Parachurch staff you have *personally* known have been
   ☐ generally positive toward the local church
   ☐ generally negative toward the local church

5. Do you believe that parachurch organizations are making a significant contribution to the kingdom of God today?
   ☐ Yes   ☐ No   ☐ Some are   ☐ Most are not

6. Have you or your church had positive experiences with parachurch staff?   ☐ Yes   ☐ No
   Example:

7. Have you or your church had negative experiences with parachurch staff?   ☐ Yes   ☐ No
   Example:

8. Please list the major problems you feel the parachurch movement presents today:

9. Do you see any theological differences between parachurch organizations such as seminaries, denominational associations and organizations, schools, and mission agencies as opposed to groups like Campus Crusade for Christ, The Navigators, and Jews for Jesus, etc.?   ☐ Yes   ☐ No
   Comments:

10. Do you like to have parachurch staff as part of your congregation?   ☐ Yes   ☐ No
    What percentage of your congregation is involved in parachurch groups?   ☐ Under 5%
    ☐ 5-10%   ☐ 10-25%   ☐ Over 25%

11. Do you think there is a proliferation of too many parachurch groups?   ☐ Yes   ☐ No
    Comments:

12. What do you think has caused the formation of so many parachurch groups?
    Comments:

13. Biblically, do you believe in "storehouse tithing"?
    ☐ Yes   ☐ No

14. Do you feel that the parachurch movement is a major drain on *your* church's income?
    ☐ Yes   ☐ No

15. In your church, do you have people who were influenced by parachurch groups for salvation or personal growth?   ☐ Yes   ☐ No

16. Were you either personally led to Christ or helped in a significant way by a parachurch group?
    ☐ Yes   ☐ No
    Which group? _____

17. Do you feel the "electronic church" is different from other parachurch groups?   ☐ Yes   ☐ No
    If yes, in what ways? _____
    _____

18. How can local congregations or parachurch groups serve each other and work together better?
    Comments:

19. Please share any other comments or ideas you may have on the subject of the relationship between the local church and parachurch organizations:

20. Please list any books, papers, or other references
    you think would be helpful in this research:

THANK YOU!

PARA-LOCAL CHURCH LEADERS' SURVEY
The Local Church and the Para-Local Church

Name: _____ Position: _____

Organization: _____

Address: _____

1. If you lead a denominational organization or association, do you regard your organization as a parachurch ministry or not?
   Comments:

2. In what ways does your organization relate its ministries to the ministries of local churches?
   Comments:

3. If your organization trains men and women for leadership responsibilities, can you document how your organization has contributed to the leadership and ministries of local churches?
   Comments:

4. What are some of the other ways in which you seek to relate your ministry to the ministries of local churches?
   Comments:

5. Please describe the ways you expect your staff to relate themselves to local churches:

6. How can parachurch groups and local churches
   serve each other and work together better?
   Comments:

7. Does your organization contribute financially to
   any local church ministries?
   Example:

8. Please share any other comments or ideas you may
   have on the relationships between parachurch organizations and local churches:

9. Please list any books, papers, or other references
   you think would be helpful in this research:

THANK YOU!

Bibliography

Allen, Roland. *Missionary Methods: St. Paul's or Ours?* Grand Rapids: Wm. B. Eerdmans Publishing Co., 1962.

_____. *The Spontaneous Expansion of the Church.* Grand Rapids: Wm. B. Eerdmans Publishing Co., 1962.

Baker, Nathan Larry. "Baptist Polity and Para-Church Organizations." *Baptist History and Heritage,* July 1979, pp. 62-73.

Bayly, Joseph. "Reigning Fat Cats and Dogs." *Eternity,* June 1979, p. 55.

_____. "Checks and Balances." *Eternity,* November 1980, pp. 57-60.

Board, Stephen. "The Great Evangelical Power Shift." *Eternity,* June 1979, pp. 17-21.

Bright, William. "Campus Crusade and the Church." *Worldwide Challenge,* May 1982, pp. 7-19.

Commission, Conflict, Commitment: Messages from the Sixth Annual International Missionary Convention. InterVarsity Press, 1962.

Cook, Harold. "Who Really Sent the First Missionaries?" *Evangelical Missions Quarterly* 12 (1975): 233-39.

DeJong, James A. "Parachurch Groups." *The Banner,* 10 June-15 July 1977.

Durant, Will. *The Story of Civilization.* Vol. 4: *The Age of Faith.* New York: Simon & Schuster, 1950.

_____. *The Story of Civilization.* Vol 5: *The Renaissance.* New York: Simon & Schuster, 1953.

_____. *The Story of Civilization.* Vol. 6: *The Reformation.* New York: Simon & Schuster, 1957.

Engstrom, Ted. "Is Overhead a Waste of Money?" *Eternity,* April 1976, pp. 24-25.

Etychus and His Kin. "The Offense of a Parachurch Ministry." *Christianity Today,* 6 October 1978, p. 6.

Glasser, Arthur. *Theological News and Notes,* October 1981, p. 7.

Guder, Darrell L. "What Can Young Life Learn from the Church?" Institute of Youth Ministry, *Occasional Papers,* April 1979.

Hales, Edward J., and Youngren, J. Alan. *Your Money / Their Ministry.* Grand Rapids: Wm. B. Eerdmans Publishing Co., 1981.

Henry, Carl F. H. "Preparing to Serve the Church." *Christianity Today,* 6 February 1981, p. 23.

_____. "The Road to Eternity." *Christianity Today,* 17 July 1981, p. 30.

Hutcheson, Richard G. "Crisis in Overseas Mission: Shall We Leave It to the Independents?" *The Christian Century,* 18 March 1981, pp. 290-96.

_____. "Pluralism and Consensus Mainline Church Mission Budgets Are In Trouble." *The Christian Century,* 6-13 July 1977, pp. 618-24.

_____. "Where Have All The Young Folks Gone?" *Christianity Today,* 6 November 1981, pp. 33-35.

"Interview: Jerry Ballard." *United Evangelical Action,* Summer 1980, pp. 11-14.

Jacquet, Constant H. *Yearbook of American and Canadian Churches.* Nashville: Abingdon Press, 1982.

Kantzer, Kenneth S. "Love of God Demands Love for His Church." *Christianity Today,* 17 July 1981, pp. 14-16.

Latourette, Kenneth Scott. *A History of the Expansion of Christianity.* 7 vols. Grand Rapids: Zondervan Publishing House, 1970.

Lindsell, Harold. "The Decline of a Church and Its Culture." *Christianity Today,* 17 July 1981, p. 35.

MacDonald, Gordon. "Taking Potshots at the Pastor." *Christianity Today,* 17 July 1981, pp. 52-55.

MacDonald, William. *Christ Loved the Church.* Kansas City, Kan.: Walterick Publishers, n.d.

Marty, Martin E. "Denominations Surviving the '70s." *The Christian Century,* 21 December 1977, pp. 1186-88.

Mellis, Charles J. "Voluntary Societies as Communities: Insights from Rufus Anderson." *Missiology* 6 (January 1978): 91-96.

Murphy, Edward F. "The Missionary Society as an Apostolic Team." *Missiology* 4 (1976): 101-18.

"Parachurch Fallout: Seminary Students." *Christianity Today,* 6 November 1981, pp. 36-37.

"Parachurch Groups: A Report on Current Religious Movements." *Discipleship and Worship Program.* New York: United Presbyterian Church in the U.S.A., n.d.

Peters, George W. *A Biblical Theology of Missions.* Chicago: Moody Press, 1972.

_____. *A Theology of Church Growth*. Grand Rapids: Zondervan Publishing House, 1981.

Radmacher, Earl. *What the Church Is All About*. Chicago: Moody Press, 1978.

Richards, Lawrence O. *A New Face for the Church*. Grand Rapids: Zondervan Publishing House, 1970.

Richards, Lawrence O., and Hoeldtke, Clyde. *A Theology of Church Leadership*. Grand Rapids: Zondervan Publishing House, 1980.

Richards, Lawrence O., and Martin, Gib. *A Theology of Personal Ministry*. Grand Rapids: Zondervan Publishing House, 1981.

Sanny, Lorne C. "The Unity and Diversity of the Church." *The Daily Walk* (Navigator edition), July 1982.

_____. *"You* Are Called to the Ministry." *The Daily Walk* (Navigator edition), August 1982.

Schaeffer, Francis A. *The Church at the End of the 20th Century*. Downers Grove, Ill.: InterVarsity Press, 1970.

_____. *The Complete Works of Francis Schaeffer*. 5 vols. Westchester, Ill.: Crossway Books, 1982.

Shelley, Bruce L. *Church History in Plain Language*. Waco, Tex.: Word Books, 1982.

Snyder, Howard A. "The Church as God's Agent in Evangelism." In *Let the Earth Hear His Voice,* pp. 337-42. Minneapolis: WorldWide Publications, 1974.

_____. *The Problem of Wineskins*. Downers Grove, Ill.: InterVarsity Press, 1975.

_____. "Why the Local Church Is Becoming More and Less." *Christianity Today,* 17 July 1981, pp. 66-70.

Sweeting, George. "First, the Good News." *United Evangelical Action,* Fall 1981, pp. 16-18.

Tillapaugh, Frank R. *The Church Unleashed.* Ventura, Calif.: Regal Books, 1982.

Van Gelder, Craig. "Local and Mobile: A Study of Two Functions." Paper, Reformed Theological Seminary, Jackson, Miss., 1975.

Wagner, C. Peter. *Church/Mission Tensions Today.* Chicago: Moody Press, 1972.

_____. *Church Growth and the Whole Gospel.* New York: Harper & Row, 1981.

Wilson, Ron. "Parachurch: Becoming Part of the Body." *Christianity Today,* 19 September 1980, pp. 18-20.

Wilson, Samuel, ed. *The Mission Handbook: North American Protestant Ministries Overseas.* 12th ed. Monrovia, Calif.: MARC, 1979.

Winter, Ralph D. "The Anatomy of the Christian Mission." In *The 25 Unbelievable Years.* Pasadena, Calif.: William Carey Library, 1970.

_____. "The Two Structures of God's Redemptive Mission." *Missiology* 2 (1974): 121-39.

_____. "Protestant Mission Societies: The American Experience." *Missiology* 7 (1979): 139-78.

"Young Life Reaches Out to Church It Once Bypassed. *Christianity Today,* 4 September 1981, pp. 74-75.

Youngren, J. Alan. "Parachurch Proliferation: The Frontier Spirit Caught in Traffic." *Christianity Today,* 6 November 1981, pp. 38-41.

Scripture Index

Subject Index